The
Meaning
of
Truth

The Meaning of Truth

by

ALVIN R. DYER

Consisting of:

The Meaning of Truth

The Kingdom of Evil

The Day of the Gentile

Published by

DESERET BOOK COMPANY

Salt Lake City, Utah

1961

Printed by

DESERET NEWS PRESS

in the United States of America

INTRODUCTION

The preparation of the manuscripts which eventually provided the material for the three articles of this book, (A) The Meaning of Truth, (B) The Kingdom of Evil, and (C) The Day of the Gentile, resulted from talks given to missionary and other groups. Publication of them was sought only after frequent requests made by listeners for the material. Even then they would not have come to print had it not been for the frequent importuning of my missionary son Brent and wonderful daughter Gloria who felt that others would enjoy the thoughts expressed in them. Thus this book is dedicated to them.

There are many wonderful things about the gospel which do not always seem clear. Answers to these, while not affecting our individual pursuit of salvation, can nevertheless provide enrichment of thought and purpose, actually motivating to the living of a better Christian life.

The thoughts given in treating these three subjects have led many to a greater appreciation of the glorious gospel plan which daily expands before our very eyes.

There can be no other purpose, in the preparation of this material than to provide incentive in the lives of those who read its contents. Incentive to respond to the knowledge that there is a God chosen people and incentive to live in the light of that knowledge.

THE AUTHOR

Section One

The Meaning of Truth

The Meaning of Truth

For those who read and attempt to understand the Holy Bible it will be found that the meaning of "truth" is not made clear. This is unfortunate, for the truth as proclaimed by the Lord, when it is understood and adhered to, makes available to mankind the way of eternal life. The interrogation of the Christ by Pontius Pilate as he stood before him, accused by the Jewish high priests, approached an answer, but as the record is given it was not clarified by the Christ upon this occasion, nor in any part of the known ancient Holy Scriptures.

The instance at which Pilate made the interrogation of Christ, is given by the Apostle John:

> Pilate therefore said unto him, Art thou a king then? Jesus answered, Thou sayest that I am a king. To this end was I born, and for this cause came I into the world, that I should bear witness unto the TRUTH. Everyone that is of the truth heareth my voice.
>
> *"Pilate saith unto him, WHAT IS TRUTH? . . .*[1]

The scriptural account, which continues, simply states that after this question was asked, Pilate went out again to the Jews and proclaimed that he could find no fault in Jesus. But the question as to "truth" was not answered. Perhaps an early manuscript containing the answer was lost or perhaps the answer which Christ must have invariably given was not recorded.

At any rate, the Prophet Joseph Smith centuries later, acting under the inspiration and revelation from this same Lord, who stood before Pilate, declared by revelation, the meaning of "truth" in these words:

> And truth is knowledge of things as they are, and as they were, and as they are to come;[2]

---

[1] John 18:37-38.
[2] D&C 93:24.

Truth, therefore, is eternal and unchangeable. A truth declared today is the same as it would have been declared centuries ago, had there been an occasion to declare it. A truth made known in our own time, cannot be at any variance with the truth written in ages past; or even upon some far-off planet rolling in the depths of space. Truth is eternal; it will ever be found applicable, no matter when or where given, to that law upon which it is predicated. Furthermore, should a truth be discovered by so-called scientific approaches, or given by divine revelation through a prophet of God, each in its own sphere of influence, the period of its announcement, whether or not it is understood by man, is not consequential, it must ever remain as a truth and will circumvent all error and simply stand as a truth.

The differences of concept between men of science and those of religion, with regard to the origin, purpose, and destiny of man and of his present abode, the earth, or of the universe, continue in our own so-called enlightened age. While apparently devoid of physical violences, which once characterized the disputes, the evident controversy of word and concept is perhaps more pronounced today than at any other time in the world's history.

Definitions

Science, briefly so stated, is a pursuit of knowledge operating through the intelligence of man in the constant seeking and finding of eternal truths that pertain to man, the earth, and the universe.

Religion, in the true Christian concept, depends upon revelation from God for its faith and teachings of truth. These teachings, because of God's concern for the human family, often involve certain fundamental truths of life, which may be sought after and found by strictly scientific pursuits. Religion is actually a science, for the true follower of the Christ will ever seek after truth. He may not look for it in test tubes or nuclear reactors, but from pure knowledge as it will be revealed from God unto his servants, the prophets.

When any fundamental truth is established, either by scientific pursuits or by direct revelation from God, there could be no disputes, or actual variances, for the source of the knowledge is the same. Whether man receives a knowledge of truth by divine revelation or through the workings of science, in the realms of which he is capable, where gradually is understood the application of the same truth, the result will ever be the same.

There will never come a time when God will reveal unto his servants any knowledge that is contrary to law, "for all things abideth the law of its own kingdom"—consequently when and if science discovers a *truth,* it will harmonize with the will of God, if such is given, in the revealed declaration of the applicable law.

Not All Religious or Scientific Statements Are True

It should be remembered, that not all statements made by those professing knowledge through either scientific or religious pursuits, are necessarily true. Just the opposite has been in evidence throughout the ages of the past. When religious leaders or institutions supposedly relying upon inspirational sources for information through revelation have made statements of error, it must be conceded that such error is devoid of any divine direction. Science likewise in its many erroneous calculations must concede faulty channels of information and lack of complete knowledge in arriving at conclusions, and become, as Paul the ancient apostle, told Timothy, "Science falsely so called."

When dealing with the universe and the earth upon which man lives, or of any physical law, whether it be science or religion, truth is the governing factor; the simple deduction, therefore, is that when either announces a truth, there should be no cause for variance.

References herewith are taken from the book, *Gospel Philosophy* by J. H. Ward, (pp. 21-27) out of print now, but finding application in our own day, we read the following:

A conflict has been going on for years between some students of science on one side and the devotees of religion on the other. Nearly all the great and good men of the medieval or modern times have been engaged on one side or the other, and a hard contest it has been. The war has been waged longer, the battles have been fiercer, the sieges more persistent, the diplomacy more far-reaching, and the revenge more deadly than ever characterized the great military campaigns of Alexander, Caesar, or Napoleon.

It will be recalled by those acquainted with history, that the first great conflict between science and the so-called Christian church of that time was in reference to the geography, the shape, and the surface of the earth. When science disclosed the fact that the earth is round, there was a great commotion in all Christendom, since the discovery was made by Mahometan and Jewish scholars. This declaration was particularly aggravating to the Christians of that day who were led to say,

Is it possible for vile Mahometans to understand and teach such a truth when it is not yet known to the assumed church of God?

But here arose the difficulty: the so-called Christian church by apostasy had lost the key of revelation. Her decisions depended not upon the voice of inspiration but upon musty parchmental teachings of an erroneous past. Claiming to be the church of God, she regarded her decisions as infallible and irrevocable, her teachings as beyond question, her ideas were crystallized; her philosophy, if indeed it was worthy of that name, was stationary.

Upon this announcement concerning the earth's geography, at once the war spirit became fierce and hot. The great writer Eusebius treated the doctrine with contempt. Lactantius asks,

Is there any one so senseless, as to believe that there are men whose footsteps are higher than their heads? That the crops and trees grow downward? That the rains, snow and hail fall upward to the earth?

At this stage of the controversy, Cosmas Indicopleustes, by direction of the Catholic church, undertook to give a description of the earth. According to Cosmas, the universe is in the form of an immense box, twice as broad as it is high and twice as long as it is broad. At the bottom of this box lies the earth surrounded by four great seas or oceans. At the outer edges of these seas rise immense walls, which support the vault of heaven, even as the walls of a house support the roof; and thus walls and vault shut in the earth and all of the heavenly bodies. This vast box he divides into two compartments or stories. In the lower one men were said to live and sun and moon and stars to move. The upper one was said to be the abode of God and the angels, whose principal work was to move the sun and planets to and fro and to open the windows of heaven and thus regulate the quantity of rain. Cosmas arrived at his theory concerning the earth by specific references of various scriptures from the Holy Bible.

Scriptures Misinterpreted to Support Erroneous Theory

When we investigate the scriptures which Cosmas used to support his theory, it can well be realized how readily one who is not inspired or who does not have the key whereby the truths of biblical statements are to be correctly understood can be misled into false and utterly untrue statements. These scriptural references which Cosmas used are given herewith.

As to the Four Seas Surrounding the Earth

And God said, let there be a firmament in the midst of the waters, and let it divide the waters from the waters.[3]

_____
[3]Genesis 1:6.

As to the Pillars or Walls Supporting the Vault of Heaven

The pillars of heaven tremble and are astonished at his reproof.[4]

As to the Rains or Waters That Were Held to Deposit upon the Earth

Praise him, ye heavens of heavens, and ye waters that be above the heavens.[5]

As to the Separation of the Heaven from the Earth

It is he that sitteth upon the circle of the earth, and the inhabitants thereof are as grasshoppers; that stretcheth out the heavens as a curtain, and spreadeth them out as a tent to dwell in.[6]

The controversy regarding the earth does not particularly exist today, but one might well wonder, at the time when this description was given, the source of the supposedly true knowledge of the geography of the earth, advanced by the Catholic Cosmas, and other Christian leaders who at that time freely supported his theory as a fundamental fact. How do we explain their lack of true inspiration?

It is seen here, that the supposed church of Christ devoid of revelation declared an untruth, while the scientist with intelligence of man enlightened by the Spirit of God, had discovered a truth.

Time will not permit here to follow this contest in all of its phases. Sufficeth it to say that so late as the fourteenth century Cecco d'Ascoli was burned alive for asserting his belief in the roundness of the earth. The students of history will also remember how Columbus at the great council of Salamanca was overwhelmed by texts of scriptures wrested from their rightful meaning, presented

---

[4]Job 26:11.
[5]Psalm 148:4.
[6]Isaiah 40:22.

at that court by learned priors, attempting to prevent his intended and, later to be, history-making voyage.

Because of such errors as were sustained by the so-called Christian church, it must be conceded, therefore, in a scientific not less than a religious point of view, that many leading minds looked with favor toward that great religious movement known as the Reformation which was to break the bands of bigotry and false concepts.

Second Great Controversy

While Luther, Calvin, and Zwingli were busy denouncing the corruptions of the Romish church, the forces were preparing for the *second great conflict between science and so-called religion, namely that concerning the motion of the earth.*

We are indebted once again to J. H. Ward for the thoughts contained in his book, (pp. 26-32) contributing to the following statements of this historic controversy.

Copernicus, a Polish scientist, born at Torun, Poland, but who leaned to German allegiance, lived at the same time as Luther and died two years before him. His was as brave a life as ever lived in history. For thirty-six years, at the very time the Protestant struggle was raging, he was working on his immortal book in which he so clearly demonstrates the motion of the earth, and the revolution of the planets around the sun. But he dared not print it for many years. If he published it at Rome, it would fall into the hands of the Inquisition; if he caused it to be printed in Germany, there were the Protestant leaders no less hostile; if he sent it to Switzerland, there stood Calvin and Zwingli ready to burn it. At length the work was ready for the press. By the entreaty of rebellious Romish Cardinal Schomberg, and with many apologies, Copernicus ventured to publish it. He was now old and feeble, while patiently he waited at death's door to see a printed copy. At length the long looked for copy arrived. He saw it, composed himself, and died in the year 1543.

Seven years after the death of Copernicus, was born that strange individual, Giordano Bruno, who advocated and taught the principles found in the book from Copernicus concerning the rotation of the earth around the sun. He had to flee to Switzerland, but Calvin held power there, and Bruno was soon obliged to leave. Driven in succession from England, France, and Germany, he ventured later to return to Italy. He was arrested in Venice and after eight years of solitary confinement was burned in Rome, February 16, 1600. When the atrocious sentence was passed upon him he nobly replied,

Perhaps it is with greater fear that you pass this sentence upon me than I receive it.

Meanwhile Galileo was prosecuting his studies at Florence. In May of 1609 he made his first telescope, and pointing it toward the heavens saw the satellites of Jupiter, and the phases of Venus. These were two of the weightiest arguments that had yet been presented in favor of the Copernican Theory. Already Galileo began to encounter vulgar indignation which accused him of impiety. In 1611 Galileo publicly exhibited the spots on the sun. This only excited the rage of his persecutors. Goaded by opposition he wrote a letter in 1613 to Abbe Castelli, showing that the scriptures were given for our salvation and not to teach astronomy in particular. This was repeating Bruno's offense. Galileo was brought before the Inquisition and after years of imprisonment only saved his life by denying the great truths he had discovered. He died in 1642 in the seventy-eighth year of his age, the prisoner of the Inquisition; but religious bigotry did not end there, it tried to follow him beyond the grave disputing his right to make a will and denying him burial in consecrated ground.

Unfortunately the leaders of the Protestant cause were no less bitter, for though these men, Luther, Calvin, Zwingli, and others, had protested against the irrevocable and assumed infallible and false teachings of the Romish

NICOLAVS COPERNICVS TORNÆVS BORVSSVS MATHEMAT. NAT. ANNO 1473 OB 1543

Non docet inſtabiles Copernicus ætheris orbes,
Sed terræ jnſtabiles arguit ille vices.

Historisches Bildarchiv Handke — Bad Berneck NICOLAUS COPERNICUS
(1473-1543)

church, yet they themselves exhibited the same spirit against those who would dare announce a truth contrary to their concepts.

In reference to Copernicus, Luther, the great reformer, without the inspiration of revelation declared this,

> People give ear to an upstart astrologer, who strives to show that the earth revolves.
> This fool (Copernicus) wishes to reverse the whole system of astronomy.[7]

Zwingli declared this,

> The earth can be no where, if not in the center of the universe. It is a part of a good mind to accept the truth as revealed by God, and acquiesce in it.

Here we see the lack of inspiration which these two men, great as they were as reformers, had concerning these truths. Calvin further proved the darkness of his own mind when he put to death that celebrated philosopher, and physician, Michael Servetus, *whose greatest crimes were that in religion he denied the absurd dogma that the Father, Son, and Holy Spirit are three separate and distinct beings and are yet one and the same person,* and in science he had partially succeeded in discovering the circulation of the blood. The circumstances were also of the most atrocious character. Servetus was roasted for two hours in the flames of a slow fire made of green wood. *And thus the superstitions and bigotry of the Protestants were not far behind that of the Catholics.* In the presence of the Protestant king, James the First of England, it was declared that Agnes Sampson with two hundred other witches had sailed in sieves from Leath to North Betwick Church to hold a banquet with the devil. It was also said that witches had baptized and then drowned a black cat, which caused a terrible storm in which the ship that carried the king narrowly escaped being wrecked. King James and the high church dignitaries who formed his

---
[7]*Idem.*

privy council believed the accusation and condemned the poor woman to flames.

The leaders of German Protestantism were Luther and Melanchthon, yet even they were victims of the grossest superstitions. They believed that in the Tiber, not far distant from the pope's palace, a monster had been found having the body of a man, the head of a mule, and the claws of a bird of prey. After much speculation and searching of their Bibles they concluded it was a manifestation of God's anger against Rome, and they wrote a pamphlet about it.

Protestantism therefore itself, as time went on, proved its weakness as a system of reform since it took up, in many instances, the very tools of iniquity which plagued those of the early Christian church.—Thus, it may be well not to extol the leaders of this movement as warriors of reform unduly for they, too, were men of their times.

When we read of Copernicus escaping persecution only by death, of Bruno burned alive as a monster of impiety, of Galileo imprisoned and humiliated as the worst of misbelievers, we are forced to look upon these things as the effects of religious institutions entirely devoid of revelation and inspiration from God.

No Differences between True Science and True Religion

Another controversy, between religion and science, age-old in its concept, continues in our day with all its bitterness. This involves the creation of man and the forming of the earth. But, in these vital issues, as in all conditions where *truth* is involved, when the facts are fully known, the revelations from God to his servants the prophets will be subscribed to by the true findings of men. True religion and true science will always be in harmony. *The source of knowledge is the same,* and from which source could never come conflicting concepts.

The Light of Inspiration unto All Men

In 1832 there was revealed unto the Prophet Joseph

Historisches Bildarchiv Handke — Bad Berneck MICHAEL SERVETUS
(1511-1553)

Smith, the source of this knowledge as it pertained to man and the universe.

> And the light which shineth, which giveth you light, is through him who enlighteneth your eyes, which is the same light that quickeneth your understandings;
> Which light proceedeth forth from the presence of God to fill the immensity of space—
> The light which is in all things, which giveth life to all things, which is the law by which all things are governed, even the power of God. . . .[8]

Similar reference to this power is made in the teachings of the Apostle John concerning the power and administrative mission of Jesus Christ whom he refers to as the "Word."

> In the beginning was the Word, and the Word was with God, and the Word was God.
> The same was in the beginning with God.
> All things were made by him; and without him was not any thing made that was made.
> In him was life; and the life was the light of men.
> And the light shineth in darkness; and the darkness comprehended it not.[9]

Thus, it is ruled by the Lord, in this enlightened age, made possible by the restoration of the Gospel of Truth, that man, by the application of intelligence, may find out many great Truths. The prophet or authorized representative of God upon the earth, in addition to this source of inspiration, however, will have also the bestowals of divine truths directly given, through the intercession of instruction and revelation made by messengers sent from the presence of God or by an open manifestation.

Benefits of Science

Science, that process or pursuit to find out truths about man and the universe, must never be underrated. As a civilization we owe much to science for on every

---

[8] D&C 88:11-13.
[9] John 1:1-5.

side we see its benefits. The food we eat, the clothes
we wear, and the houses we dwell in depend a great
deal upon it. Our travel by land, sea, or air are by the
mechanisms of science. The so-called Jet Age can be
nothing but a tribute to the intelligence of man, enlightened as it is by the light or inspiration of Truth,
administered by the Spirit of God. The books we read,
the illumination to read by, the conveniences of our
homes, and the super highways we travel on, have come
by scientific advancement. The relief of human suffer-
ings, the saving of lives through medicine and research,
the promotion of human happiness, all are affected by
and owe much to science. God has so ordained by
the dissemination of light and truth that man shall find
out many things for himself, and these discoveries when
correctly established only serve to prove the governing
laws of such which God himself has established.

The Age of Enlightenment

It has been estimated that ninety percent of all the
scientists that ever lived upon the earth are alive today.
Scientific advancements in our modern age can be explained by the revealed fact, that the restoration of the
gospel, and the "pouring out" of God's Spirit upon all
flesh, in this last dispensation of God's will, known as the
fulness of times, is producing an influence of enlightenment upon all flesh. Thus, through God-given intelligence, man can discover the laws that pertain to the
universe and man. This was announced by the Prophet
Joseph Smith,

> . . . that I may bring to pass my strange act, that I
> may pour out my Spirit upon all flesh—[10]

The Prophet Joel spoke anciently of this very same
condition in the latter days, when great intelligence would
fill the earth, reacting to the discovery of many of the
strange and great things of life,

---

[10]D&C 95:4.

> And it shall come to pass afterward, that I will pour
> out my spirit upon all flesh; . . . your old men shall
> dream dreams, your young men shall see visions:[11]

It will be of interest, to those who may be concerned, to categorize and analyze scientific achievements in virtually every field, since the time of the restoration of the gospel of Jesus Christ through the Prophet Joseph Smith, in 1820, thereby indicating the fulfilment of the prophecies made by him and others many years before these many discoveries were made.

Men of research and science who have that vision to project their thought and action into the channels of truth, will find inspiration in accordance with God's promise of inspiration. It is to be hoped that their findings will be used for the good and blessing of mankind, not their destruction.

Revelation—Divine Personal Appearance Greater

In addition to this source of inspiration in a manner more emphatic and far-reaching, the prophets and authorized servants of God will have the bestowals of divine truths directly given, through the intercession made by messengers sent from the presence of God or even the appearance of Holy Deity, to give instruction or in announcing divine Truth intended for man's salvation.

Scientific Concepts a Part of the Gospel in All Ages

When the true Church of Jesus Christ exists upon the earth, whether as in the Meridian of Time, or anciently, as in the days of Adam or the religion of Jehovah, referred to by the apostle Paul as the Gospel, which before was preached in the days of Moses and Abraham, or as it is now proclaimed in this the Dispensation of the Fulness of Times, restored in these last days through the instrumentality of the Prophet Joseph Smith, there are basically no conflicts arising between its fundamental teachings and the true findings of science.

---

[11]Joel 2:28.

Men of God Anciently Were Scientists

In ancient times, as can be observed by the writings
and declarations of the prophets Moses, Job, David, Abraham, Isaiah, and others, these great men themselves were
the leading scientists of their time. They understood, to
an advanced degree, natural history, architecture, sculp-
ture, music, botany, and astronomy. In the latter they
made such progress in their findings, that many of the
constellations still retain the names which they used,
such as Orion and Pleiades.[12] Moses and Abraham among
these perhaps rose to the most eminent level in their
knowledge of man and of the universe, a fact established
by the translations of the Book of Abraham and revelations contained in the Book of Moses, in the Pearl of
Great Price.

Scientific Truths Known by the Prophets of God

In the third chapter of Abraham, in the Pearl of Great
Price, many important truths, regarding the planets and
stars, as they were made known unto Abraham, a prophet
of God in ancient times, are herein made known to the
Prophet Joseph Smith in this dispensation of time, by virtue of a divine gift of translation which enabled him, a
revelator, to understand certain Egyptian hieroglyphics
that had fallen into his hands.

The Prophet Joseph Smith, from time to time, declared many fundamental scientific truths, so recognized
by the world, not in the sense of complete technical
coverage, but in statement-like form, the validity of which
would tend all the more to prove that its issuance was
divinely inspired. For here, without the preponderance
of usual information that would normally cover such a
declaration, had it been made in a so-called scientific
manner, a scientific fact is made known. Yet this announcement will stand as the truth, and cannot be refuted.

This would indicate, that now, as in times of old,
both religious and scientific truths are given unto the

12Job 38:31; Amos 5:8.

prophets of God. In fact, in the strict sense of the true meaning of both, there is no difference. A prophet of God is in very deed a true scientist.

Evidences of Joseph Smith's Scientific Knowledge

With regard to a scientific statement being declared by a prophet of God, consideration is given here to several that have been proclaimed by the Prophet Joseph Smith. These having come from the fountainhead of knowledge, are indisputable. As the years come and go, and as science is able to uncover the truth, regardless of conflicting concepts, it will be found that her findings will subscribe in every way to prophetic announcements. Recent findings of science have already given its corroboration of these facts.

These declarations are submitted herewith in outline form only:

(1) *Matter in whatever form is eternal.*

For man is spirit. The elements are eternal, . . .[13]

Comment:

Here a great truth is declared in referring to the eternal nature of the element of which the mortal body is composed, and which needless to say, also refers to all matter or element. It is the very law which makes possible the resurrection of the mortal body, that it may inseparably be united with the spirit, which itself is an element and is also eternal.

This truth concerning the non-destructibility of matter, while declared in connection with a great spiritual principle, is finding scientific substantiation every day. Many times there have been men who have thought that matter could be destroyed, only to find that it had changed its form. The most recent of scientific statements concerning matter, is that it is an energy, electrical or otherwise. The chain reaction in the exploding of the atomic

---

[13]D&C 93:33.

or hydrogen bombs has served to prove how impossible
it is to destroy a basic element such as plutonium. Scientists may change its form, yes, but never destroy its locked-
up power. The elements are eternal, and of an eternal
substance is made the species of God and man, who are
of the same order, for man is in the express image of God.

The amazing developments of science in this field
led the now deceased, brilliant Einstein to say that he
could not hope to understand the properties of energized
matter.

In the discourse of B. H. Roberts on the "Protest
against a Dying Universe," some few thoughts of interest
are gathered.

> There was a time when learned men felt reasonably
> secure, for instance, in the thought that matter was in-
> destructible. Also that energy was indestructible; that
> while these existences might change forms, the substance
> of the things was perpetuated, and the universe was
> secure as an enduring thing. But the new knowledge,
> recently developed in the years indicated, (since 1900)
> has changed all that, and men are saying today that
> matter is being destroyed; that energy is radiated away,
> and that the whole universe is imminently in danger, with
> a lapse of time, of absolute annihilation.[14]

This theory of a dying universe and the complete
destruction of matter, if true, would nullify the statement
of the Prophet Joseph Smith and prove him a false prophet
and therefore no prophet at all. But in the light of still
later findings, eminent scientists express supporting evidence to the declaration of the Prophet Joseph Smith. One
of such will suffice to give evidence of the fact, that when
science has developed the truth about the matter, their
findings will support the declarations of the Prophet of God.

> Dr. Millikan, against the contentions of most of his
> conferees in science, holds that the cosmic ray is so power-
> ful, though its source is unknown as yet, that it will
> have the power to convert the radiated matter and

---

[14]B. H. Roberts—Seven Last Discourses.

energy of the universe back to mass, and establish the
eternity of the universe.

William L. Laurence in his report on Dr. Millikan's
representations of the Cosmic Ray at the National Academy
of Sciences at Pasadena in late September of 1930, said:

> Dr. Millikan has gone far afield in the development
> of a new cosmology based on the results of these further
> experiments with the cosmic ray. This new cosmology
> has its central point in the hypothesis that the creation of
> worlds and all matter is a never ending process that goes
> on today and will go on forever.[15]

(2) *The Law of the Species.*

> And the Gods organized the earth to bring forth the
> beasts after their *kind,* and cattle after their *kind,* and
> every thing that creepeth upon the earth after its *kind;*
> and the Gods saw they would obey.
> And the Gods took counsel among themselves and
> said: Let us go down and form man in our image, after
> *our* likeness; and we will give them dominion over the
> fish of the sea, and over the fowl of the air, and over
> the cattle, and over all the earth, and over every creeping
> thing that creepeth upon the earth.
> So the Gods went down to organize man in their own
> image, in the image of the Gods to form they him, male
> and female to form they them.[16]

Comment: (Reference, J. H. Ward, *Gospel Philosophy,*
pp. 187-191)

While Darwin, Huxley, Hooker, Spencer, and others
revealed to the world a vast amount of knowledge concerning the origin of the species and the development of
plants and animals, there were those who would have
gladly found an antagonism between the facts of science
and the records of revelation. But now it is admitted that
it would be equally wonderful, would as much require
the infinite powers of Deity, to develop all the varied
and marvelous forms of organic life from a single germ
as to call them into existence by special acts of creation. In

---

[15]*Idem.*
[16]Pearl of Great Price, Abr. 4:25-27.

reality we owe these philosophers a debt of gratitude for having studied nature so carefully and given us so many deeply interesting and important facts.

It is evidently a part of the divine plan that species should develop from a lower to a higher condition. We see this in the improvements in the breeds of our domestic animals, as well as in wild animals that now live, as compared with the remains of the ancient Saurians that once roamed over the earth. The doctrine of "Natural Selection" or "Survival of the Fittest," as Huxley terms it, is also a law of nature. We see this illustrated at the present time in the history of the races of men and species of animals. The weaker races of men are gradually disappearing while those nations who possess the highest mental, physical, and moral characteristics are extending their dominion over the earth.

The lion, tiger, bison (or buffalo), elephant, rhinoceros, and, in fact, all the fiercer and larger animals, are even now disappearing before the advance of civilized man.

The law of variation, as expressed by Darwin, is true with certain limitations. For example, every person must admit a vast change in the condition of the best breeds of our domestic swine, from their ancestors, the wild boars of medieval Europe. *Yet nowhere can be found a single trace of transmutation of species.* For example, if we should trace the pedigree of the horse backwards through a thousand generations we should find that the original animal was also a horse, though probably a very inferior animal.

Of all the living animals and fossil remains of extinct ones, though thousands of specimens have been found, yet of land animals and the higher orders of creation, not a single instance of transmutation can be found.

True, we are told by Huxley that the embryos of different animals closely resemble each other, so that at an early state of their existence they cannot be clearly distinguished. But what of this? It only shows the unity of design in the works of the Creator which is one of the grand characteristics of the world. Further, it teaches us a lesson of man's ignorance and lack of knowledge. With all the aid of science we are unable to perceive those minute arrangements of atoms or basic cells from which growth emanates, which will on development produce a tortoise or a fowl, a dog or a man. Who will presume to say that a castle was developed or "evolved" from a cottage because they were built of the same materials or because some of the rooms were after the same pattern? Why then should the Divine Architect's work be doubted because he gives to the germs of different beings the power of self-development according to a specified pattern, which is to the end of a vastly different organism, each in ultimate perfection?

Early Man

The "primeval savage" is a common idea, and the so-called learned never tire of presenting to us a primitive man as only a little above the brutes, devoid of knowledge, art, language, or culture, a creature in few respects, elevated above, but mostly beneath the anthropoid apes, from whom, it is contended, is his descent by way of evolution.

In the maze of supposedly learned presentations, it is contended by Rawlinson, one of the great students of ethnology, and in his own right a celebrated scientist, that there is absolutely no proof of this supposed priority of savagery to any form of civilization.[17] This fact likewise is simply stated by a prophet of God, Joseph Smith, that all things mineral, animal, and human remain in the sphere of its creation.

The hypothesis of evolution is, therefore, a viewpoint of man, which endeavors to show how man has been brought from one state of growth to another; from the ape to the savage and thence to a creature of a higher human order resulting, thus far, in the human specie which we view today. But when we listen to the voice of God's

---

[17]George Rawlinson, *The Origin of Nations*, p. 2.

prophet with regard to the spirit and intelligence that have been placed in the physical body of man, which has been created for that purpose, then we realize how weak and shallow and vain are the imaginations of man as he attempts to explain the wonders of God's plan in the pro-creation of man. The Prophet Joseph Smith, by revelation, received the following enlightenment,

> There never was a time when there were not spirits; for they are co-equal (co-eternal) with our Father in heaven.
> God never had the power to create the spirit of man at all. God himself could not create himself.
> The mind or the intelligence which man possesses, is co-equal (co-eternal) with God himself.[18]

Spirits of Men Graded

As to the gradation of men's spirits, as they are placed into a human form, the Prophet states the following,

> . . . if there be two spirits, and one shall be more intelligent than the other, yet these two spirits, notwithstanding one is more intelligent than the other, have no beginning; they existed before, they shall have no end, they shall exist after, for they are . . . eternal.[19]

The glorious plan of life and salvation, involving the peopling of an earth, to provide man with the opportunities of further growth, in the true manner of evolution, as has been revealed to the Prophet Joseph Smith, indicates the purposes of God, "to bring to pass the immortality and eternal life of man." In the light of such knowledge, the foolish theories of man, to place the glorified spirit intelligence of man, which is in the form and image of God into a base and low form of life, and then endeavoring to trace its ascendancy, provides a most irrational application of man's God-given intelligence.

The Growth or Evolution of Man in His Own Sphere

The truth of man's growth within the sphere of his

---

[18]*Teachings of the Prophet Joseph Smith* (J. F. Smith) pp. 353, 354.
[19]P. of G. P., Abraham 3:18.

existence, is an acknowledged fact. For man is constantly improving himself, this is the very plan of life and salvation which God intended for his spirit children as they sojourn in this life. And it will not end here. The transitions of man's development upon the earth can easily be followed, and these are attributed to many known reasons. The Greeks for example, are known to have passed from a semi-savage state, as described by Homer, to that of a high civilization.

The Romans, gradually exchanged their low form of life known to them in the 8th Century B.C., for the splendor of the Augustine age. The growth of these and other respective civilizations can be found to stem actually from a retrogression, from that of a state of prior existence; for example, in the days of Adam, Enoch, or Abraham when knowledge and intelligence were poured out upon man, the pursuits of life were gentle and progressive. Yet contemporary with these periods, were people who were hardly civilized, the history of whom, it is clear, reveals that they had turned away from God and the light of truth.

It is not difficult to trace some of these retrogressions. Take, for instance, the Arab hordes issuing from the desert, unkempt, dirty, and almost naked, with no literature but the Koran, no art but that of the forging iron. These we can trace back to the glories of the Baghdad caliphate and the magnificence of Granada.

A certain degeneration of the Jews can be traced from the post-Babylonian period to the time when the Davidic power held sway. Likewise we see the degenerating effects of time on the descendants of the once mighty Romans, of the Dacians, or of the Trojans.

In our own land of the Americas, as recorded in the Book of Mormon, we see the degeneration of a once proud and gifted and delightsome people, to that of a degenerated race, killing and being killed, even down to the last man, but who beforehand, as savages, submitted themselves to a satanic blood worship in the sacrifice of maidens on the altars of their false gods.

Retrogressions Point to Mistaken Periods of Prime Savagery

Another striking example of the degeneration of a race of people, who are now in retrogression are the "Weddas" of India, now practically extinct. This tribe of people is so debased as to be considered virtual savages. Their language is limited to some few hundred vocables. They cannot count beyond 2 or 3. They, of course, have no idea of letters, they have domesticated no animal but the dog, their arts consist of making bows and arrows, they have no idea of God, and scarcely any memory. In height, they rarely exceed five feet and are considered degenerate both mentally and physically.

Yet, the best comparative philologists pronounce their language to be that descended from the most elaborate, and earliest known form of Aryan speech, the Sanskrit. The Weddas are believed to be descendants of the Aryans, who overcame the Dravidians and occupied India. The Aryans of that time can be considered as having possessed a reasonable state of civilization.[20]

Thus, on the whole, there would seem to be grounds for believing broadly that savagery and civilization, the two opposite poles of our human civilization, are states between which men oscillate, as internal and external circumstances bear pressure. The observance of a savage race at its low ebb, may to some be sufficient grounds to contend our earth life antiquity, from degenerate to generate. It must be admitted by all, however, that the records and actual authentic information we have disprove this, and that all early pictures of life upon the earth portray a high state of civilization.

There were no savages in the Garden of Eden. The high state of intelligence of our first parents enabled them to learn quickly how to prepare themselves clothing, and to learn and practice early the two main modes of life,

---

[20]George Rawlinson, *The Origin of Nations*, p. 7.

namely, pastoral and agricultural. The slow and laborious steps in the development of man, as contended by others, are not in evidence here. They were in likeness, in their earth life body to that of their Creator, and were blessed with great perception: cities were built and the riches and blessings of earth life soon came under their domination. The earliest-known civilizations all seemed to follow this pattern.

Thus the declaration by the Prophet Joseph Smith, concerning the order of creations, remaining in its own spheres, while not given in a so-called scientific manner, declares with solid firmness the truth, that never, worlds without end, could there be a transmutation of species, for each order of growth, each kingdom of creation, must remain in its own sphere of life. The eternal laws governing this principle are immutable. Science, as it learns more of these laws, will subscribe to the declarations of the Prophet Joseph Smith.

(3) *The Planets and the Stars*

> And worlds without number have I created; and I also created them for mine own purpose; and by the Son I created them, which is mine Only Begotten. . . .
> . . . For behold, there are many worlds that have passed away by the word of my power [earth life to glorification—celestialized]. And there are many that now stand, and innumerable are they unto man; but all things are numbered unto me, for they are mine and I know them.[21]

Scientific findings confirm, almost daily, the truth of these statements uttered by the Prophet Joseph Smith.

In writing of our own galaxy, (or Milky Way, of which our earth is a part) Fritz Kahn in his book, *Design of the Universe*, states the following:

> According to mathematical reasoning, the total mass of the Milky Way should be 250 Billion Stars. Yet statistical calculations, based upon photographs of different parts of the Galaxy point to the fact that not more than

---
[21]P. of G. P., Moses 1:33, 35.

200 billion radiant stars are gathered in our Galactic
System. About one-fifth of our total mass must, therefore,
exist in invisible form as dark clouds or dark stars,
of planets of these stars, as moons of these planets, or as
planetoids, meteors, cosmic dust, or thinly distributed
gases.

With regard to the immensity of space, and a finite
concept even, of the eternal nature of God's creations, we
read further:

Not only are stars not crowded, they are terrifyingly
isolated in space. The Milky Way could encompass a million times as many stars without being "filled up." The
chances of one star colliding with another, even in the
densest section of our Milky Way, are only one in 500
trillion years.[22]

Conclusion of Scientific Declarations by the Prophet

Other scientific inferences made by the Prophet Joseph
Smith with attendant proof could be given, but these three
will suffice to illustrate the fact, that, when a prophet of
God speaks and his utterances encompass certain allusions
to conditions incident to the true purpose of man and the
universe, such utterances will always be found in harmony
with the facts which men of science may uncover.

True Religion of Christ
(The Gospel)

Statements have been made in this article, that true
religion and true science could never be at variance. To
qualify this statement we must identify "true religion" as to
mean the Church of Jesus Christ which has been divinely
bestowed and founded upon apostles and prophets, wherein
the channels of revelation from God are open for divine
direction. Such a religion must provide man with the
means, (a Plan of Salvation) whereby through obedience
to the laws and ordinances given, he can return to the
presence of God having thus obeyed all and having fulfilled the measure of his birth into this life.

-----
[22]Kahn, *Design of the Universe,* pp. 157-158.

In this sense therefore, the religion which is referred
to, that cannot be just "any religion" is primarily interested
in the salvation of the human race. Those who have gone
before, who are here now, or who will yet come. Revelation given to God's prophets, having to do with basic truths,
other than covenants and principles of redemption, will of
necessity be confined to this planet upon which man resides.
This, it would seem, is objective to the purposes of God in
the saving of men's souls in this life and in this sphere of
action. This understanding was made known to the
Prophet Joseph Smith.

> For behold, this is my work and my glory—to bring
> to pass the immortality and eternal life of man.
> And now, Moses, my son, I will speak unto thee
> concerning this earth upon which thou standest; and
> thou shalt write the things which I shall speak.[23]

Should it be the desire, however, of God to speak directly of the planets and worlds which surround us, of
which man has but a meager understanding, it would be
a simple matter, for they are known to him. The laws
which govern them are under his control from the great
planet Kolob, which planet, in the orbit of its function,
is set close unto the throne of God.

Better to Know Principles of Salvation

In the light of this knowledge, which refers to space,
time and occupied planets with the laws by which they
function, and with the further knowledge that God, our
Heavenly Father, is the ruling power over all of them and
the source of all light and knowledge, (D & C 88) how
then, could there be any logical dispute between science
and true religion, if and when the truth of both are known
and compared.

Because of the fact, that a knowledge in completeness,
of the planets at this particular time, *is not* necessary to
the salvation of mankind, only fragmentary statements have

---

[23]P. of G. P., Moses 1:39, 40.

been given rather than a complete understanding of the laws governing them. These statements have appeared as incident to other purposes of the various revelations.

It is a fact, therefore, as far as revelation to a prophet of God is concerned, that complete information has been withheld until a later time, when in the wisdom of God such should be made known to man, by divine intercession.

Man may, of course, continue to sweep the heavens with his telescope, develop newer and greater uses of nuclear power, find out more about the functioning of the human mind and body, and develop new ways of combating diseases which shorten man's sojourn here upon the earth and in many other ways continue his endless search for knowledge, which without question will result in benefits to mankind. All of these things God will permit and has ordained, in accordance with the eternal law of agency of thought and action, which is the motivating force of life. But all that man shall find out in the application of the sciences, is already known unto God in infinitely greater proportions, which greater understanding, if he deemed it wise could be bestowed upon man, and conveyed to his intelligence in less time than it would take to build one telescope, cyclatron reactor, or atom furnace.

But God has not willed it so, at least not yet. Thus man will continue his search, cumbersome and slow though it may be, and as he unveils each golden truth, it will ever harmonize with the laws and declarations of God. Yet God does not oppose, nor does the true Church of God oppose the scientific search for the physical laws of life and the universe.

The Importance of the Saving of Men's Souls

In matters, however, pertaining to the souls of men and the plan of redemption, God has ruled it otherwise. In this noble pursuit, it is not his will, that the things of God should be left to the sciences—where man in and of himself, could find these things out simply by a systematic study, to uncover the truths of redemption. Such a method of search could only lead to despair and confusion. For the things of God cannot be understood by the physical logic and reasoning of man only. Efforts to do this very thing have led to devious Christian societies, which for lack of revelation from God, teach for commandments the doctrines of men.

Of necessity, to save his own children, God turns to divine intercession by means of revelation, to his servants the prophets, that mankind may know, by doctrine, commandment and ordinance, the Truths necessary for his redemption.

Knowledge the Possession of the Noble Ones

Needless to say, however, it is interesting to contemplate the great strides that could be made in the sciences, were it possible to have access to the fountain of knowledge, in the same manner that the principles of life and salvation are revealed to his prophets. For that which man strives to learn by earthly scientific methods, pertains to laws already established and well known by our Father in heaven and other noble personages of the pre-earth existence.

The laws of space travel, advanced nuclear chemistry, principles of power in magnetic force, and many other laws are known and used to an ultimate degree by the exalted ones. Were the elements of their knowledge conveyed unto the men of science today, it would move their acquisition of knowledge ahead a thousand years, perhaps a million, who knows the extent of heavenly knowledge. But, supposing these things were revealed to man, what would be the advantage? How would it benefit him in the search for the truths that he should learn from this earth-life existence necessary to equip him for the life to follow this one? Is it not infinitely more important that the divine laws of salvation and exaltation be given him here that he may successfully keep this estate, and thus be enabled to go forward to the next, or sub-mortal estate, having accomplished the real purpose and intent of this life. It is so, and thus God in his great wisdom, has spoken directly to his prophets, for the best ultimate good of man, to provide for him that which he could never learn for himself without divine intercession.

It is so simple to declare, as we view science and religion in this manner, that there can be no logical quarrel between these two, for they shall ever meet on common ground when the *truth* is known.

The Pursuits of Science Not Displeasing to God

In connection with the pursuits of science, it is interesting to call attention to the fact, that God intends that man shall continue his independent search for truth. This is made known on a facsimile in the Book of Abraham in the Pearl of Great Price, which portrays in ancient custom, by symbolical sign writing, events of importance pertaining to the life of man, and of the Creator.

This particular facsimile indicates the place of Kolob, the governing planet, and of Oliblish which stands next to Kolob, in the government of the planets which belong to the same order as the earth.

God sitting upon his throne is also typified, with the cross of eternal light upon his head, representing the keys of the Holy Priesthood.

The earth is also represented, as also many other things of great interest. Some of the figures and symbols on the facsimile have not at this time been revealed. Yet, *the world* (represented by science) *may find them out if they can!*

The information provided on the facsimile, is from an inspired translation by the Prophet Joseph Smith. It indicates the fact that God is not adverse, nor is the Church, to men obtaining as much knowledge as they can by scientific research.

"For let them find out these things, if they can"

A FACSIMILE FROM THE BOOK OF ABRAHAM

No. 2.

EXPLANATION OF THE FOREGOING CUT

Fig. 1. Kolob, signifying the first creation, nearest to the celestial, or the residence of God. First in government, the last pertaining to the measurement of time. The measurement according to celestial time, which celestial time signifies one day to a cubit. One day in Kolob is equal to a thousand years according to the measurement of this earth, which is called by the Egyptians Jah-oh-eh.

Fig. 2. Stands next to Kolob, called by the Egyptians Oliblish, is the next grand governing creation near to the celestial or the place where God resides; holding the key of power also, pertaining to other planets; as revealed from God to Abraham, as he offered sacrifice upon an altar, which he had built unto the Lord.

Fig. 3.   Is made to represent God, sitting upon his throne, clothed with power and authority; with a crown of eternal light upon his head; representing also the grand Key-words of the Holy Priesthood, as revealed to Adam in the Garden of Eden. as also to Seth, Noah, Melchizedek, Abraham, and all to whom the priesthood was revealed.

Fig. 4.   Answers to the Hebrew word Raukeeyang, signifying expanse, or the firmament of the heavens; also a numerical figure, in Egyptian signifying one thousand; answering to the measuring of the time of Oliblish, which is equal with Kolob in its revolution and in its measuring of time.

Fig. 5.   Is called in Egyptian Enish-go-on-dosh; this is one of the governing planets also, and is said by the Egyptians to be the Sun, and to borrow its light from Kolob through the medium of Kae-e-vanrash, which is the grand Key, or, in other words, the governing power, which governs fifteen other fixed planets or stars, as also Floeese or the Moon, the Earth, and the Sun in their annual revolutions.   This planet receives its power through the medium of Kli-flos-is-es, or Hah-ko-kau-beam, the stars represented by numbers 22 and 23, receiving light from the revolutions of Kolob.

Fig. 6.   Represents this earth in its four quarters.

Fig. 7.   Represents God sitting upon his throne, revealing through the heavens the grand Key-words of the Priesthood; as, also, the sign of the Holy Ghost unto Abraham, in the form of a dove.

Fig. 8.   Contains writing that cannot be revealed unto the world; but is to be had in the Holy Temple of God.

Fig. 9.   Ought not to be revealed at the present time.

Fig. 10.   Also.

Fig. 11.   Also. If the world can find out these numbers, so let it be. Amen.

Figures 12, 13, 14, 15, 16, 17, 18, 19, and 20, will be given in the own due time of the Lord.

The above translation is given as far as we have any right to give at the present time.

The Restoration—The Spirit of God upon All Flesh

There can be no doubt, that many more things pertaining to life and the universe will be found out by men, inspired only indirectly as they are, by the restoration of the Gospel of Light.   But here let it be repeated once again, when found, they will harmonize with God-given truths bestowed upon the prophets by direct revelation. There can be no doubt as to the day and age in which we are living being an age of enlightenment.   Great and marvelous things shall come forth as a result of the intelligence of man.   The reasons for this contemporary greatness, with manifestations being made to the prophets, and of their divine bestowals, can be seen in the declarations that have been made by both ancient and modern prophecy. The Prophet Joel spoke of this, referring to our particular time.

> And ye shall know that I am in the midst of Israel, and that I am the Lord your God, and none else: and my people shall never be ashamed.
>
> And it shall come to pass afterward, that I will pour out my spirit upon all flesh; . . . and I will shew wonders in the heavens and in the earth.[24]

In a revelation given to the Prophet Joseph Smith we read the following, which undoubtedly refers to this same condition in the last days when all flesh shall benefit in an over-all way, from the restoration of the Gospel of Light.

> For the preparation wherewith I design to prepare mine apostles to prune my vineyard for the last time, that I may bring to pass my strange act, *that I may pour out my Spirit upon all flesh—*[25]

(Strange Act i.e.: A Marvelous Work and a Wonder.)

The Relationship between True Religion and the Free Agency of Man

The religion established by Jesus Christ will never interfere in the exercise of the God-given gift of free agency. This, man must have to fulfil his destiny, upon this earth, as a spirit child of God. The force of unrighteous dominion will never be invoked by the true Christian church. The violation of this sacred principle is clearly seen in many of the pursuits of the post-apostolic Christian church. This fact alone, if for no other reason, should cause the sincere investigator of truth to weigh carefully, any and all doctrines, systems of religious procedure and professed authority, stemming from such an institution.

The Prophet Joseph Smith, emphasizing this principle gave the following,

---

[24]Joel 2:27-30.
[25]D&C 95:4.

We claim the privilege of worshiping Almighty God
according to the dictates of our own conscience, and
allow all men the same privilege, let them worship how,
where, or what they may.[26]

Through the portals of "unjust dominion" could never
come the truth, to save and redeem mankind. To preserve
and invoke this sacred right upon man in this mortal life
as a necessary element of salvation, a conflict took place
in our pre-existent sphere, wherein certain forces of that
estate led by Lucifer, a prominent spirit, sought to destroy
the free agency of man. This situation, which occurred prior
to our mortal life, is clearly spoken of, and apparently
well understood by the prophets and teachers of both the
Old and New Testaments. In these references, it can be
seen that Lucifer, a son of the morning, sought to invoke
a plan covering the second estate of man, (earth life) that
would deprive him of his free agency, and thus make of
him a thing to be acted upon, rather than to have the
power to exercise his own volition, in all things pertaining
to his life.

How art thou fallen from heaven, O Lucifer, son of
the morning! how art thou cut down to the ground,
which didst weaken the nations![27]

The Apostle John, the beloved of the Christ who was
permitted to tarry in the flesh of his mortal body until the
second coming of his Master, saw in panoramic view the
events pertaining to this life, in glorious vision while confined a prisoner under the ruler Domitian on the Isle of
Patmos. He gives a description of the fall of Lucifer, and of
his expulsion from the presence of God, by reason of his
aggrandizement and attempt to change the eternal law of
free agency.

And there was war in heaven: Michael (Adam) and
his angels fought against the dragon; and the dragon
fought and his angels,

---

[26]Eleventh Article of Faith.
[27]Isaiah 14:12.

And prevailed not; neither was their place found any more in heaven.

And the great dragon was cast out, that old serpent, called the Devil, and Satan, which deceiveth the whole world: he was cast out into the earth, and his angels were cast out with him.[28]

From the revelations given unto the Prophet Joseph Smith the full meaning of this event is made known,

Wherefore, because that Satan rebelled against me, and sought to destroy the agency of man, which I, the Lord God, had given him . . . I caused that he should be cast down.[29]

The Power of Evil Continues

From the beginning of man's mortal probation here upon the earth, men have sought, under the influence of this same spirit of rebellion, fostered by Satan or Lucifer, by the use of the dominion of force to suppress men's rights and free agency, to gain personal and political ascendancy. Unfortunately, this same power of unrighteous dominion has been exercised by the church in the post-apostolic period, evidencing, therefore, the lack of its divine inspiration.

Wherever force is imposed by institutions, governments, or churches, it can have but one course of motivation, regardless of how it is colored to appear otherwise—that of evil. Such motives have never been, nor ever will be, in harmony with the commandments of God.

This glorious principle descends upon us with all the majesty of its intent, in a revelation from God to the Prophet Joseph Smith.

Verily I say, men should be anxiously engaged in a good cause, and do many things of their own free will, and bring to pass much righteousness;

For the power is in them, wherein they are agents unto themselves.[30]

---

[28]Rev. 12:7-9.
[29]P. of G. P., Moses 4:3.
[30]D&C 58:27-28.

But Satan, not entirely defeated in his pre-existent encounter, and permitted, by the will of God (Rev. 12th Chapter) to provide opposition for mankind here upon earth,

> For it must needs be, that there is an opposition in all
> things.[31]

Satan continues his warfare against the forces of truth and righteousness here upon the earth. His methods are the invoked principles of deception, unjust dominion and force, which he practices upon all who become prey to his enticings. Therefore, the stifling of men's rights, the subjugation of the right of agency, in whatever degree, or by whomever it is invoked, becomes a part of Lucifer's plan to deceive the world and frustrate the plan of God.

A Fallacy of Truth

One of the indications, that the so-called post-apostolic Christian church was and is an apostate church, can be seen in the fact that it has and does now apply the unjust principle of force in its attempt to stifle agency and freedom of thought of man.

This fallacy of principle, as it was invoked, in the realm of its influence, led not only the early Christian Church into the depths of a still greater apostasy, internally, but through the dissemination of such principles of error imposed upon the world a period of abject darkness, for over one thousand years from which the world did not awaken until the beginning of the thirteenth century. From here came the awakening, the revival of learning. Men began to throw off the shackles of force and deception. This period is referred to in our history as the Renaissance.

The post-apostolic Christian church opened its doors to false philosophies of men and pagan customs and teachings as a means of spreading its influence. This is abundantly attested to by authentic historical records. These

---

[31] 2 Nephi 2:11.

measures were effective, and Christianity began to rise as a new epoch. In justification of the infiltration of error into the early Christian Church as a means of converting the heathen, we note the following from the writings of Cardinal John Henry Newman, who admits the compromise with existing philosophies, and violations of pure Christian principles, to thus satisfy the pagan masses.

> Confiding then in the power of Christianity to resist the infection of evil, and to transmute the very instruments and appendages of demon-worship to an evangelical use, and feeling also that these usages had originally come from primitive revelations and from the instinct of nature, though they had been corrupted; and that they must invent what they needed, if they did not use what they found; and that they were moreover possessed of the very archetypes of which paganism attempted the shadows; the rulers of the Church from early times were prepared, should the occasion arise, to adopt, or imitate, or sanction the existing rites and customs of the populace, as well as the philosophy of the educated class.[31]

The compromises of thought however did not extend to science, and as the power of the church increased, a glacial-like freezing was clamped upon science. Referring to the causes of the "Dark Ages," Fritz Kahn, in his book, *Design of the Universe,* states the following:

> Intellectualism (science) in its most modern form was despised. The only ones who read and wrote, also modestly were the priests and monks who became the guardians of the spiritual heritage of antiquity. The cultural relics were by no means studied or venerated, but were regarded with suspicion and pity, as the works of a still unenlightened humanity.
>
> Science, independent of the Bible slept for a thousand years.—Then came the slow, slow awakening called the Renaissance, the age of re-birth.[33]

Fritz Kahn calls attention to the fact also, that during this period, one single book was venerated as the source

---

[32]*Essay on the New Development of Christian Doctrine—Great Britain,* V 1878, chapter 8, p. 269.
[33]*Design of the Universe,* p. 7.

of all truths. It was the authentic encyclopedia for all natural sciences.

In the face of the interpretations given to the writings of the Holy Bible by the early Christian leaders in the period of our subject, (Cosmos—geography of the earth) devoid of divine revelation, it is no wonder that men of science could not, and do not to this day understand and appreciate the true meaning of the writings of the prophets.

The Holy Bible, or that compilation of scriptural writings, containing only part of that which had been written and preserved in antiquity, is truly a marvelous record and contains the teachings of eternal life; although in the possession of those who misinterpret its true meaning, it can induce confusion and misunderstandings. The true patterns of life must be known to apply its sacred writings. The post-apostolic church, without divine revelation, could not teach its message.

The first fallacy of the early apostate church can be summarized in the fact, that, the so-called Christianity, that emerged from the Dispensation of the Meridian of Time (i.e., the period of Christ and the apostles) imposed in false manner, many detriments upon the civilization through which it functioned.

Intellectualism, while not that of true science, rather of science falsely so called, as declared by the Apostle Paul to Timothy, was responsible, to a large degree, for the inroads made into the early Christian Church, which produced an entirely different Christianity from that which the Christ and the apostles intended. The evidences of this are clearly discernable from the writings of the apostles, who struggled against this man-made force, while they were yet living, which force of evil set out both within the church as well as without, to nullify the simple pure teachings of the Master, for something more paganistic and cultural, as was associated with the philosophies of the time.

Perhaps an anxiety and zealousness, on the part of the apostles to extend the saving principles of the Gospel unto all, attracted unto the Church many who did not come in by the spirit of conviction; perhaps too many were intellectually converted, as they were swayed by the masterful teaching of Paul and others. This new sect, they thought, would provide the means of expression of their own philosophies.

Had these early would-be brilliant converts been truly in harmony with the teachings of Christ, it would have meant much to this young and struggling faith, but their widespread campaigning for the inclusion of pagan teachings and customs, philosophies of the would-be Greek immortals, together with many heretical doctrines and a complete renunciation of priestly authority, undermined the true Church and eventually produced an apostate church.

The simple truth of the matter was that the apostles were fully aware of what was taking place, but seemed helpless to stem the tide. Their Master, the Christ, had predicted it. The revelation which they received concerning this condition led to their profuse prophecies concerning "the falling away" and final apostasy of the entire Christian body.

A few of such apostolic predictions are submitted:

> But there were false prophets also among the people, even as there shall be false teachers among you, who privily shall bring in damnable heresies, *even denying the Lord* that bought them. . . .[34]

> I marvel that ye are so soon removed from him that called you into the grace of Christ unto another gospel:

> Which is not another; but there be some that trouble you, and would pervert the gospel of Christ.[35]

(See also 2 Thess. 2nd chapter, re: Falling Away)

This false suppression brought the "dark ages," and imposed upon an apostate people a grim judgment. "Ye

---

[34]2 Peter 2:1.
[35]Gal. 1:6-7.

shall know the truth, and the truth will make you free," a declaration of the Master, found no application in this period of darkness.

This, it is contended, was a fallacy of the post-apostolic Christian church. And, just as it was wrong in this pursuit, so was it wrong in other practices and teachings.

The institution of religious reforms with Martin Luther and others in the fourteenth century, was but the beginning of the awakening of man to the need of the truth concerning life and salvation. In this, those who protested against Catholicism, recognizing its falseness, came face to face with the reality of providing the real. The surge of men's thoughts moved forward in this direction. But, not finding the answer adequately, or of being able to assure themselves of the complete truth, there arose fragments of truth, based upon the *best efforts* that man could put forth to understand the divine will of God, as it may be invoked in the establishing, once again, of *the true Christian church.*

Thus arose many Christian sects, each claiming to be the true church, but, each different in its concept, with not any uniting with the other to form one great church of the reformation, or of the new truth. The very nature of these protests, that moved in different directions, casts a shadow over their authenticity. They knew the Catholic church was wrong, but they had not the revelation or divine intercession to establish the truth as Christ would have it.

Nevertheless, this great period of reform, produced in men's thinking the desire to know the truth, with the courage and daring to reach out in search of it. Such a spirit spreading over mankind was intended to prepare the way for the coming of the restoration, with its attendant divine bestowals. But the noble men of the reformation played their parts well. They were foreordained to protest, *not to restore.*

The Reality of a Prophet of God Receiving Revelation Today Is Baffling to the Human Mind

Unfortunately, men of science and others find it difficult to accept the reality of God's revealing his mind and will, in announcing great truths through a prophet today. Some refer to such an occurrence today, the very day that they live in, as too fantastic and unscientific to believe. Unfortunately, a scientist becomes very unscientific when he closes his mind to the channels of truth made possible by revelation through a prophet of God, from the source of all knowledge—*GOD*. Others, particularly those of professed belief in Christ, have been heard to say, "God is through with speaking to prophets. He may have revealed his mind and will to them anciently, and through his Son Jesus Christ, but things like this simply cannot happen now."

Thus, the false reasoning of the human mind, both in and out of religious circles, precludes the credibility of the declarations of the Prophet Joseph Smith. But aside from the fact as to whether or not Joseph Smith saw God and his Son Jesus Christ, the results of which led to subsequent appearances of divine messengers sent from the presence of God enabling him to declare unto the world great religious truths that have a direct bearing upon the salvation and exaltation of man, aside from this fact, and there are ways that all this can be tested as to its truth, *Why should it be considered a thing incredible that God would manifest himself? Why is the idea scoffed at by so many, when it is realized that God is the Father of all spirit children that enter into earth-life bodies, and surely can select his own time and place and through whom he will speak unto his children?* God is the Author, through his Son Jesus Christ, of the plan of life and salvation, who would, therefore, attempt to confine his mind and will, in revealing to his children, the truths necessary for their own redemption.

Repelled by the New Idea and Truth

Perhaps the failure of mankind to accept the concept
that God has spoken to a prophet in this period of time,
to correct erroneous concepts of life and salvation, can be
found in their inability to adjust to the "new idea" concept
of things. Yet it has always been a fact in every phase of
life, that when the truth is known and accepted, tremendous benefits have resulted for the good of man.

The Christ once proclaimed,

And ye shall know the truth, and the truth shall
make you free.[36]

The basis of this declaration is the eternal answer to
those who would reject "new ideas," forbid investigation,
and even in many cases deny to any man *the right to investigate for himself*. Yet against powerful and formidable
evidences of *truth*, or "the new idea," as they put it, men
have arrayed themselves and have been unwilling to yield
to the inspiraton of God's will as it is made manifest,
through a chosen prophet. Often, because men are deceived, where they otherwise might accept *the truth*, they
are turned against it.

Evidences of Men's Unwillingness to Adjust

Even in material things the world opposes new truth.
When England began using spinning machinery that saved
thousands from grinding toil, giving employment at better
wages with easier work to hundreds of thousands, it was
necessary to protect the new machines inside of stone
walls. Workmen hated the new idea and would wreck the
machinery.

When steamships made of iron were first suggested,
all those who supposedly knew anything about shipbuild-
ing denounced the idea as foolish. The public joined in,
"What idiocy to talk about a ship of iron. It is hard enough

---
[36]John 8:32.

to keep a wooden ship afloat. Nothing will keep an iron ship from sinking." Yet, today nearly all are made of iron (steel).

The railroad was also denounced; even the intellectually brilliant Ruskin opposed what has now become one of man's greatest material benefits. It was thought then the constant speed of twenty miles an hour, hour after hour, would ruin the beautiful countryside, and the concussion of such speed would kill those along the road. Many continued to invest their money in stagecoaches.

The sewing machine was attacked outrageously. The first inventor was persuaded by his wife to break the model, because it would take employment away from anyone who earned her living with a needle. Actually it has saved millions of women from slavery.

Hatred of the "new idea" was never so vigorously displayed as when attacks were made upon scientific discoveries that have proved beneficial to man. When the idea of vaccination for smallpox—a disease now almost extinct—was first suggested, some clergymen said, "It was flying in the face of providence." Reverend Edward Massey preached against it. "Job's distemper," he declared, "was probably smallpox and doubtless the devil inoculated him."

Most amazing of all was the statement that, "Diseases are sent by Providence for the punishment of sin, and attempting to prevent them is a diabolical operation."

When Dr. Boylston vaccinated his own son in Boston about 200 years ago, a clergyman urged the authorities to try him for murder, declaring that "Smallpox is a judgment of God on the sins of the people, to avert it is to provoke Him more."

Men of old, and men of our day, have hated "new ideas" for many reasons. First, the "new idea" compels the brain to think and adjust; this sometimes is difficult. Secondly, the "new idea" threatens established ways. The steam engine replaced stage coaches; the telephone did away with a majority of the messenger boys. The auto-

mobile and the airplane are interfering now with rail
traffic. Whoever is disturbed, opposes the disturber. And
the *new idea*, like a bright light in a dark place, always
disturbs somebody.

The idea of the acceptance of great spiritual truths,
long hidden from the world, as proclaimed by Joseph Smith
the Prophet, acts as a disturber upon many, because it
requires a change, from that which they have previously
believed and accepted. The teachings of antiquity, in so
many instances false, are so erroneously rooted, that men
are deceived and blind to the truth, and when it is presented to them, they simply oppose the idea, of the change
of concept, regardless of its truth and eternal benefits.
Thus, men hate new ideas to their own retarding of progress.

In our own day, we have learned by hard lessons the
value of progress. The discoveries of new things are more
common and readily acknowledged. But, unfortunately,
this applies only to physical things, such as may be seen
and participated in by the physical senses. The lesson of
spiritual perception still comes hard, as men continue to
resist the effort of a loving Father in heaven to bestow
upon them, through an authorized servant, or prophet, the
principles of truth needed for their spiritual, and conse-
quent eternal advancement.

Our Own Day and Time

We are living in a day of great progress, of change,
of rapid advance. The very structure of our civilization,
social, political, commercial, moral, and religious, is greatly affected by that which persists before our very eyes.

There can be no question that a new era has dawned
upon our planet. Means of travel, trade, association, and
inter-communication between countries, even compara-
tively unknown, is before us.

While in almost every field of science, every art is
being developed—while the mind is awakened to new
thought, religious knowledge in the world is at a stand-

still. The creeds of the fathers cast in the mould of other
ages show no progress to match the onward strides of man.
Yet, as we declare it, and as fully predicted by the prophets, God has poured out his Spirit upon all mankind. As
proof of this I call upon any who are interested, to investigate the great strides made in every field of research since
1820.

How tremendously in keeping with his will, that such
enlightenment upon man should come as a result of a
restoration of truth from the very presence of God. That
which man participates in today, in scientific advancements is *minute, only a fragmentary part of the light that
has shone into the darkness,* that brings to man by divine
intervention, the truths of eternity which, if appropriated,
can lead to eternal life in the presence of God.

Joseph Smith the Prophet of the New Era

Concerning the Prophet Joseph Smith, and the effect
that the restoration of the gospel of Jesus Christ will have
upon our civilization, as recorded by those even not of
the Church, the following is submitted:

A writer for the New York *Herald,* who had visited
with the Prophet Joseph Smith in 1842, wrote the following account of his experience which was originally published in his paper:

"Joseph Smith is undoubtedly one of the greatest
characters of the age. . . . In the present infidel, irreligious,
geological, animal magnetic age of the world, some such
singular prophet as Joseph Smith is required to preserve
the principle of faith, and to plant some new germs of
civilization that may come to maturity in a thousand years.
While modern philosophy, which believes in nothing but
what you can touch, is overspreading the Atlantic States,
Joseph Smith is creating a spiritual system, combined also
with morals and industry, that may change the destiny
of the race. . . . (There is a need for) some such prophet
to take hold of the public mind—and stop the torrent of
materialism that is hurrying the world into infidelity,
immorality, licentiousness and crime."[37]

---

[37]George Q. Cannon, *Life of Joseph Smith,* p. 324.

Thomas J. Yates related an experience he had while a student at Cornell University in 1900. He had the privilege of meeting Dr. Andrew D. White, former president of Cornell, and at the time, U. S. ambassador to Germany. Upon learning that Mr. Yates was a Mormon, Dr. White made an appointment for Mr. Yates to spend an evening with him at which time he related to him an experience he had with Count Tolstoi, the great Russian author, statesman, and philosopher, while serving as U. S. Foreign Minister to Russia in 1892. Dr. White visited often with Count Tolstoi, and upon one occasion they discussed religion. We quote from Elder Yates' account of this discussion as related to him by Dr. White:

"Dr. White," said Count Tolstoi, "I wish you would tell me about your American religion."

"We have no state church in America," replied Dr. White.

"I know that, but what about your American religion?"

Patiently then Dr. White explained to the count that in America there are many religions, and that each person is free to belong to the particular church in which he is interested.

To this Tolstoi impatiently replied: "I know all of this, but I want to know about the *American* religion. Catholicism originated in Rome; the Episcopal Church originated in England; the Lutheran Church in Germany, but the Church to which I refer originated in America, and is commonly known as the Mormon Church. What can you tell me of the teaching of the Mormons?"

"Well," said Dr. White, "I know very little concerning them. They have an unsavory reputation, they practice polygamy, and are very superstitious."

Then Count Leo Tolstoi, in his honest and stern, but lovable manner, rebuked the ambassador. "Dr. White, I am greatly surprised and disappointed that a man of your great learning and position should be so ignorant on this important subject. The Mormon people teach the American religion; their principles teach the people not only of heaven and its attendant glories, but how to live so that their social and economic relations with each other are placed on a sound basis. If the people follow the teachings of this Church, nothing can stop their progress—it will be limitless. There have been great movements started in the past, but they have died or been modified before they reached maturity. If Mormonism is able to endure, unmodified, until it reaches the third and fourth generations, it is destined to become the greatest power the world has ever known."[38]

Obedient to the predictions concerning this day and age spoken of by all the holy prophets, it is not religious opinion which will cover the earth, nor knowledge from scientific advancement, reaching into the heart of every good man and woman, but it is *faith* leading to the testimony and spiritual conviction of God. God is truth. To know him is to know the *truth*.

Never, I suppose, have there been so many brilliantly intellectual people upon the earth, judged by the known facts of science and human knowledge. Eric Johnston stated recently that some ninety percent of all the scientists who ever lived are living today, and the total accumulation of scientific knowledge is doubling every ten years. *Yet, there is a tremendous lack of direction.* Recently, one of our inquiring thinkers, a noted American mental health leader, stated it this way:

Most people today live without purpose and without significance. They have no articulate philosophy, they do not live within any frame or reference.[39]

It is obvious that the lack of direction lies principally in the failure of people to have a true understanding of God and his purposes. To get this, it must come from the expressed will of God, through a prophet. Yes, a prophet today here upon the earth, as the oracle of God—and not from the corrupted concepts of a musty and deceptive antiquity—nor from a so-called "Age of Reason," imposed upon us because of scientific exploration.

God has spoken to us. Let us listen to his oracles, and have unveiled to us the realms of Eternal Life. *Here is reality.* Honest and good men must come to know this, adjust to it, welcome it, meet it as a friend and know it is God's will.

[38]*The Improvement Era*, Vol. 42, p. 94.
[39]Karl Menninger.

Opposing this great force for good, as revealed through the Prophet Joseph Smith, is the godless system of world communism, that holds many nations in its grasp, denouncing the need of religious motivation, and particularly they are opposed to the morals and virtues as taught by the Christ. (See pp. 102-103 of this book.)

The Same Spirit of Opposition to Truth

Perhaps it is this same spirit of unwillingness to accept the "new idea" concept, that stands in the way of many accepting Joseph Smith as a prophet of God. This being the fact, the world of mankind stands as the loser, because the message—given to him by Divine and Holy Personages—is intended for the benefit of the world, for so has announced the Lord!

> Wherefore, I the Lord, knowing the calamity which should come upon the inhabitants of the earth, called upon my servant Joseph Smith, Jun., and spake unto him from heaven, and gave him commandments, . . .
>
> That faith also might increase in the earth;
>
> That mine everlasting covenant might be established; . . .[40]

Every new idea or truth is opposed today, as it was yesterday and it will be so tomorrow, unless man changes his course. For whenever the truth has been made known, there have always been those who have bitterly opposed it. The calling and message of the Prophet Joseph Smith has been no exception to this pattern of human acceptance. He saw and talked with God. He thereafter received many revelations, attended also with bestowals of power, and authority from God, to minister in the ordinances of the gospel: all of this for the salvation and exaltation of mankind; if *men will but accept, and be governed by the doctrines and articles of redemption which he gave us, seeking not only intellectual advancement, but more necessarily spiritual advancement.*

[40]D&C 1:17, 21-22.

The opposition to the Prophet Joseph Smith, led him to say,

> . . . Why persecute me for telling the truth? I have actually seen a vision; and who am I that I can withstand God, or why does the world think to make me deny what I have actually seen? For I had seen a vision; I knew it, and I knew that God knew it, and I could not deny it, neither dared I do it; at least I knew that by so doing I would offend God, and come under condemnation.[41]

In announcing a truth by divine intervention, the Church of Jesus Christ of Latter-day Saints claims that an apostasy ensued following the ministry of Christ and the apostles upon the earth, resulting in a complete loss of the truths and doctrines of the Church as well as the loss of the authority, or priesthood to administer in the affairs of the church as founded by Christ. It contends further that when the true Church of Jesus Christ is upon the earth that it will be governed and controlled under the power and influence of direct revelation from God. Indeed the Church of Jesus Christ moves and breathes by revelation in which are contained the divine oracles of God for any church professing to be that of Jesus Christ can be justified only as it will move and go forward under the impetus and power of direct revelation from the presence of God.

The simple truth exists: The Prophet Joseph Smith did see God and received the divine commission that he was to be the instrument in God's hands, after the receiving of proper instruction and the conferment of the Holy Priesthood to organize and establish the Restored Church of Jesus Christ in these latter days, and in so doing provide the channels of spiritual truths to lead man back into the presence of God, our Father, in preparation for the next great state of man.

------

[41]P. of G. P., Joseph Smith 2:25.

The Truth about God

Perhaps no greater fallacy has survived the centuries, than the present-day Christian concept of God, and his Son Jesus Christ. Men have always wondered about God, as to his person or whether or not he is a person at all. Is there but one God, or are there more than one? What is our relationship to Deity? Did we ever dwell in his presence, or, will we ever? Has anyone actually seen God? —These are but a few of the questions that surge through the inquiring mind of man.

There are some, perhaps, who do not seek to inquire about God. It is contended by them that it does not matter one way or other, that in the end we will know, so, why bother about it now. Isn't it true that the complexity of a search to know the truth about God leads them to assume a passive attitude rather than to risk a state of frustration in failing to find out? Another among them has said—"If we knew or understood God he would cease to be God"— For, "How can man that is finite understand that which is infinite?"

Does not the declaration of Jesus impose upon us, however, if we would seek life eternal, *to know the truth about God.*

> And this is life eternal, that they might *know* thee the only true God, and Jesus Christ, whom thou hast sent.[42]

Joseph Smith, the great modern-day prophet, subscribes to this teaching as he tells us:

> It is the first principle of the gospel to know for a certainty the character of God; and to know that we (as Moses) may converse with him as one man converses with another.[43]

These thoughts stimulate a pursuit of a knowledge of God and suggest that in doing so man will come to know more of himself and of life eternal.

---

[42]John 17:3.
[43]*Teachings of the Prophet Joseph Smith,* (Joseph Fielding Smith) p. 345.

Let us consider the concept of God, as taught by the Christian churches of today. This can be essentially given in two statements, which will, in the main cover the generally accepted understanding, in the larger divisions of Christianity.

The following is the Roman Catholic belief,

There is but one God, the creator of heaven and earth, the supreme, *incorporeal,* uncreated being, who exists of himself, and is infinite in all his attributes, etc.

The Church of England teaches in her articles of faith,

There is one living and true God, everlasting, without body, parts, or passions; of infinite power, wisdom, and goodness.

These two statements which provide the source of the creeds for other Christian churches, plainly indicate the immateriality of God. This is found to be the orthodox notion in respect to Deity, notwithstanding it finds so many express contradictions in the scriptures.

Other definitions of a more modern concept are also presented here.

Catholic

Catholics believe in one God in whom there are three divine persons co-equal in all things. The doctrine of the Holy Trinity is a *central mystery* of the Catholic faith.

Episcopalian

God is as he reveals himself. He is creative reality (God the Father). He is expressive act, (God the Son). He is responsive power, (God the Holy Spirit). He is one God experienced in a trinitarian fashion.

Lutheran

Lutherans believe in the Trinity as one God in three personalities.

Presbyterians

Presbyterians think of God not as three individuals, but of three manifestations of one.

Methodist

The meaning of the Trinity is not fully understood, (mystery) the doctrine is the expression of the three aspects in our experience of God. The Creator, the Father; the historical personality of Christ, the Son; a pervading and continuing presence and power in our lives, the Holy Spirit. The Trinity is also the formula for understanding the personality of God. God is love which is objective in the Son through activity, with the object of his love, the Holy Spirit.

Baptist

The trinitarian formula, "in the name of the Father, and the Son, and the Holy Ghost," is used at every baptism. The sublime mystery of the Trinity, of the eternal essence of God manifested in three persons, the Baptist leaves to the theologians to interpret. He simply accepts it.

These quotations taken from the book, *The Religions of America,* published a few years ago by the University of Illinois Press from articles provided by selected exponents of the various faiths, indicate the almost unanimous declaration, that to them, God is a mystery!

One of the writers of the new dispensation approaches the inconsistency of the immateriality of God as defined by the various Christian churches from this viewpoint:

In the work of the creation, God proposed to make man in his own image and likeness, and the proposition was executed. Moreover, Jesus is said to be the brightness of God's glory, and, "the express image of his person." Again it is said, that Jesus, "being in the form of God thought it not robbery to be equal with God,"—all his teachings declare that God has a form similar to that of man's; that he has organs, dimensions, proportions; that he occupies space and has relation to other objects in space; that, as a person, he moves from place to place;

and that so far as his actual person is concerned, he cannot be in two places at one and the same instant.[44]

Undoubtedly, the idea that prevails in the Christian concept of God, that he is everywhere present, leads to a misconception as to his person. It is contended, that since God fills the universe, how could it be possible to describe him as corporeal, or having a definite form or shape?

In the light of revelation, which has been received from God, the truth concerning the omnipresence of God is made known. From the teachings of the Prophet Joseph Smith we learn the following:

> Man should know the everywhereness of God through the projection of "the light of truth," from the presence of God, which is "the same light" that quickeneth the minds of men; "which light proceedeth forth from the presence of God to fill the immensity of space. The light which is in all things, which giveth life to all things, which is the law (i.e. power) by which all things are governed, even the power of God who is in the bosom of eternity, who is in the midst of all things."[45]

This revealed statement gives clarity to the manner in which God, a corporeal personage, fills the universe and exercises a governing power over it by the projection of his presence from a focal place of administration.

To assert the immateriality of God as a substance, is not only to deny his personality, but his very existence; for an immaterial substance cannot exist. It can have no relation to time and space, no form, no extension, no parts. An immaterial substance is simply no substance at all; it is the description of an infinite vacuum.

The atheist may say, "There is no God," while the creed of God as described above simply says, "God is nothing."

Orson Pratt, a writer of the new dispensation, offers an interesting contrast between the atheist and those who

---

[44]Roberts, *Outline of Ecclesiastical History.*
[45]D&C 88.

would adhere to the belief of an immaterial God. In presenting this there is no attempt to belittle the sincerity of those who place at the altar this concept of God, their love and devotion. It is intended only to emphasize how far the concept of God has drifted from the truth.

> There are two classes of atheists in the world. One class denies the existence of God in the most positive language; the other denies his existence in duration or space. One says, "there is no God." The other says "God is not *here* or *there*, any more that he exists now and *then*."—the infidel says, "A Spirit, though he lives and acts, occupies no room, fills no space—not even so much as does the grain of sand." The atheist does not seek to hide his infidelity; but the immaterialist, whose declared belief amounts to the same thing as the atheist's, endeavors to hide his infidelity under the shallow covering of a few words.[46]

The Prophet Joseph Smith, whose great privilege it was to behold God and his Son Jesus Christ in person, has restored to mankind the truth about God. No longer need mankind grope in darkness concerning the Holy Godhead, no longer need he wonder about his relationship with Deity.

The Prophet has declared unto the world, as an appointed witness of these truths, that Jesus Christ is the Son of God. That he is divine, that man should know further that the Father and the Son are separate corporeal beings, that they are not shapeless spirits or—incorporeal phantoms. They live as separate persons in the glorious relationship of Father and Son, in whose likeness and image, we, the spirit children of the Father, have received an earthly tabernacle, resembling the body of our spirit, in stature and form, for the purpose of growth and further development in this earth-life existence which is our second estate.

Unto the Prophet Joseph Smith has been given this description of the Holy Godhead, reflecting herein also, the greatness of the power through which these beings

---

[46]*Absurdities of Immaterialism*, p. 11.

govern the destinies of man by the immutable laws of the plan of salvation:

> The father has a body of flesh and bones as tangible as man's; the Son also; but the Holy Ghost has not a body of flesh and bones, but is a personage of Spirit. Were it not so, the Holy Ghost could not dwell in us.
>
> A man may receive the Holy Ghost, and it may descend upon him and not tarry with him.[47]

This statement is intended to identify the three members of the Godhead as distinct Beings of separate proportions. And even though the Holy Ghost is a Personage of Spirit, he, too, is a separate Personage and as such, can only occupy one certain space at any given time.

In the light of that which has been revealed to man in this age of enlightenment, through the restoration of the gospel of Jesus Christ, one might well ask the question, "Whence has come this perverted understanding of the Christian God? What is the source of its creed and doctrine?"

The true answer to this question reveals the perpetuation of an antiquated doctrine of error which has compounded its effect with each passing generation.

But to those who founded this false concept must be given the responsibility for the acceptance and promulgation of a false creed about God the Father, his Son Jesus Christ, and the Holy Ghost, for the creeds found in Christian denominations today concerning the Godhead have persisted down through the centuries, and are resultant from that which was founded by an apostate church.

The Borrowed Vestige

Therefore, that which the Protestant faiths adhere to with regard to God the Father and his Son Jesus Christ, is but the borrowed vestige of that perverted creed established in error by the post-apostolic church. The teachings of a mysterious and unexplainable Trinity, continue as their

---

[47]D&C 130:22-23.

conception of God.   It is no wonder, therefore, that Jesus
spoke of these false teachings, that exist in the churches
that bear his name, who bear it no doubt with respect,
but without proper foundation of truth.

From the testimony of the Prophet Joseph Smith,
which he gave to the world, concerning the instruction
given to him by Jesus Christ in the Sacred Grove, we read
the following concerning the various Christian sects, who
were in that day seeking converts to their fold:

> . . . all their creeds are an abomination in his sight; . . .
> they draw near to me with their lips, but their hearts are
> far from me; they teach for doctrines the commandments
> of men, having a form of godliness, but they deny the
> power thereof:[48]

What appears to be a mere statement of argumenta-
tion, is in reality a far-reaching and meaningful declaration, regarding the state of the world of Christian religions
which are devoid of the Holy Priesthood with the sealing
power of Elijah, in binding the hearts of the children to
the fathers and the fathers to the children, as well as the
fact, that without divine revelation these churches were
teaching the commandments of men.

As to the source of the false creeds concerning God—
let us look in on the great controversy that developed at
the beginning of the fourth century among the various
Christian churches who were torn by conflicting theories
of the God whom they were supposedly worshiping.

From these theories or views of the Godhead can be
summarized the following categories:

> *The Orthodox View*: The view held to be orthodox
> was that in God there are three persons, Father, Son, and
> Holy Spirit: each really distinct, yet so united as to consti-
> tute one personal God—of the same substance, and equal
> as to their eternity, power, glory, and all other perfections.
>
> *Sabellius, A Bishop of a Church in Africa,* advanced
> what is referred to as the *Sabellian Theory* which held

---

[48]P. of G. P., Joseph Smith 2:19.

to the idea, that there was but one divine person in the Godhead. And that the Father, Son, and the Holy Spirit were but different aspects of the same God, and that the trinity was one of the names merely, not of distinct persons. The Logos in this theory, is an attribute of Deity, rather than a person; and its incarnation is reduced to an energy or an inspiration of the divine wisdom, which fills the soul and directed all the actions of the man Jesus.

Arius, a Bishop of a Christian Church at Alexandria, opposed the orthodox theory and maintained a real distinction in the persons of the Divine Trinity. He taught that the Son was created out of nothing by the will of the Father; and though the longest astronomical periods would not measure the time of his duration yet, there had been a time when he was not. Upon the Son thus created, the Father bestowed great glory, yet he shone only by reflected light, and governed the universe only in obedience to the will of the Father; in other words, the Son was subordinate to the Father, and was unequal in power, glory, and eternity.

The Nicene Council and Creed

It was to still the rising commotion which arose in the church through the violent discussions of these several theories, that the Emperor Constantine assembled the Council of Nicea, A.D. 325. In that council the theories of Arius were condemned, and the orthodox creed stated thus,—"We believe in one God, the Father Almighty, the maker of all things visible and invisible; and in one Lord, Jesus Christ the Son of God, begotten of the Father, only begotten, (that is) of the substance of the Father; God of God, Light of Light, Very God of Very God; begotten not made; of the same substance of the Father, by whom all things were made, that are in the heaven, and that are in the Earth; who for us men, and for our salvation, descended and was incarnate, and became man; suffered and rose again the third day, ascended into the Heavens and will come to judge the living and the dead; and in the Holy Spirit. But those who say there was a time when He (the Son) was not, and that He was not before he was begotten, and that he was made out of nothing or affirm that he was of any other substance or essence, or that the Son of God was created, and mutable or changeable, the Catholic Church doth pronounce accursed."

Athanasius, the secretary and spokesman for Alexander, a Bishop of Alexandria, a most active opponent of Arius, was called upon to give explanation to the Nicene Creed. This he did and his explanation is commonly called the Athanasian Creed. (An interesting sidelight on Athanasius: He was a young man at this particular time, of about twenty years. Historians regard him as either a Copt or an Egyptian. He was bright of countenance and was drawn to Alexander by a peculiar circumstance. From a window of a lofty house where he was entertaining other clergy, his attention was drawn to some children who were playing a strange game on the seashore. On being brought before Alexander they reluctantly confessed that they had been acting a baptism, and that one of them who had been chosen to play the part of a bishop had dipped them in the sea. Finding that the boy-bishop had administered the rite with all the proper forms, Alexander declared it to be a valid sacrament, himself added the oil of confirmation, and struck with the knowledge and gravity of the young Athanasius, he took under his charge the boy who was to be his successor. (Barker, *Protestors of Christendom*, page 72.)

The Creed of Athanasius:

> We worship one God in Trinity, and Trinity in Unity, neither confounding the persons; nor dividing the substance, for there is one person of the Father, another of the Son, and another of the Holy Ghost. But the Godhead of the Father, Son, and the Holy Ghost is all one: The glory equal, the majesty co-eternal. Such as the Father is, such is the Son, and such is the Holy Ghost. The Father uncreate, the Son uncreate, and the Holy Ghost uncreate, the Father incomprehensible, the Son incomprehensible, and the Holy Ghost incomprehensible. The Father eternal, the Son eternal, and the Holy Ghost eternal. And yet, these are not three eternals, but one eternal. As also there are not three incomprehensibles, nor three uncreated; but one uncreated and one incom-

prehensible. So likewise the Father is Almighty, the Son Almighty, and the Holy Ghost Almighty; and yet there are not three almighties but one Almighty. So the Father is God, the Son is God and the Holy Ghost is God, and yet there are not three Gods but one God.

Thus, from this inception of error, and through its continuation of acceptance in the Catholic church, as well as in the churches of the Reformation, either in direct or indirect form, can be found the reason why the Christian world, so-called as this new dispensation began to unfold and even unto this day, knew not the truth about God. Their concept of God, his Son Jesus Christ and the Holy Ghost, more or less subscribes to the creed established by the Nicean Council, held in the year of 325 A.D., in the month of June.

NOTES ON THE NICEAN COUNCIL
(From Barker, *Protestors of Christendom*)

According to Eusebius, Constantine declared that he convoked the Council at Nicea, on his own initiative, under the inspiration of God.

He provided liberally for the expenses, to and from the council, from the state treasury, for those who answered his summons to attend. Each Bishop was to bring with him two presbyters or deacons, with three servants.

To this council, impelled by various motives, came 318 Bishops. This represented about one-sixth of the total number throughout the Empire, there being about 1000 in Greek provinces and 800 in Latin. The Latin Churches sent only 7 Bishops; this fact deserves special notice, that the First Representative Assembly of all the Churches decided upon the Catholic Faith, with regard to the Creed of the Godhead, in particular, without the presence and voice of the Bishop of Rome, though the aged Sylvester was represented by two presbyters, Victor (or Vitus) and Vecentius.

The Bishops arrived in Nicea sometime in May, but the Council did not get under way until June, 325 A.D. because of the late arrival of Constantine. The opening session was held in the principal church of Nicea, but was thereafter moved to a large hall in the imperial palace.

The opening address was made by the Bishop at the right hand of Constantine, regarded by many as Eusebius, although others have thought it was Eustathius of Antioch. Constantine addressed the Council in Latin, and referred to the division in the Christian church at large with regard to the Creed of the Godhead:

> I thank God . . . Who has accorded me the grace . . . of convoking you all here. . . . The intestine divisions of the Church seem to me more serious and more dangerous than wars and other conflicts. . . . It is necessary then that your hearts be united and that peace be seen to reign among you.

Comment: It is necessary to pause here to evaluate the premise upon which the council had been called. For here within the provinces of the empire, as represented by the 1800 or more churches, were gathered together a representation of these churches, in perhaps the first general council of the church, where two patriarch Bishops of the church took a great part. (Alexander of Alexandria and Eustathius of Antioch. Alexander was recognized as to have borne the title of the Pope (Pappa or Ababba, i.e. father of fathers, or Bishop of the Bishops). They were here in council to decide on a Creed that would describe the Godhead. In boldness, it is asked, how can man decide such a truth? Why should the assumed church of God find it necessary to resort to council to determine such a truth, when it had already been revealed to them, and had it not been for the workings of an apostate people, in the whole of Christendom, the truth would still there reside, having been made known by divine revelation, which could not now or at any time be found out by the reasoning of men.

Conclusion

> For there are certain men crept in unawares, who were before of old ordained to this condemnation, ungodly men, turning the grace of our God into lasciviousness,

and denying the only Lord God, and our Lord Jesus Christ.[49]

The Persistence of False Concepts

There is no concept of things that are false, that has persisted throughout the centuries more emphatically, than the supposed Christian concept of Deity. Stemming from an erroneous past, wherein an assumed Christian body devoid of revelation and divine direction, which are truly characteristic of Christ's Church, it had founded within its body a false trinitarian doctrine which unfortunately has survived the ages with successive deception.

The fact that this concept has survived is no criterion of its validity. Other false concepts have had similar survivals. Two of these have already been referred to rather extensively in this article, which deal with two great controversies that existed between science and religion. The first of these concerned the geography and shape of the earth, while the second had to do with the revolving of the planets around the sun. Strange as it may seem, it has been the Christian bodies, who above all others should be inspired, which have fought to maintain the traditional concepts of error in connection with these two controversies.

How could this be unless, devoid of divine direction, their protestations are false and of consequence? If false in these concepts, could they not then be false in their concept of God?

------

[49]Jude 4.

Section Two

The Kingdom of Evil

FOREWORD
TO KINGDOM OF EVIL

For such are false apostles, deceitful workers, transforming themselves (self-appointment) into the apostles of Christ.

And no marvel; for Satan himself is transformed into an angel of light.

Therefore it is no great thing if his ministers also be transformed as the ministers of righteousness; whose end shall be according to their works. (2 Cor. 11:13-15.)

Does not this scripture tell us that Satan has ministers even as Christ does? Does it not state further that these Satan-inspired ministers may also be transformed as ministers of righteousness?

INTRODUCTORY COMMENT
to the
KINGDOM OF EVIL

It is apparent from the letter which the Apostle Paul wrote to the saints at Ephesus, that he was aware of the powers of darkness that constantly menaced the work of God. He likewise knew how this power, not "of Flesh and Blood" could be dealt with. His allusions to the "armour of God," no doubt, refer to the priesthood of God, which from the beginning, was given to hold in check this evil force that would attempt to destroy the efficacy of the plan of salvation, which the Father and the Son in righteousness have provided for all mankind.

The Apostle Paul knew that this power of darkness would invade the church, using the very channel of salvation, as a means of deceiving its believers. This spiritual wickedness is referred to in his letter to the wayward saints at Thessalonica,[1] and outlined quite completely in a letter to the Ephesians,

> Put on the whole armour of God, (meaning the priesthood, with its powers of leadership and administration) that ye may be able to stand against the wiles of the devil.

> For we wrestle not against flesh and blood, (i.e. things of this world) but against principalities, against powers, (governments, kingdoms, founded and maintained upon the principles promoted by the arch-enemy of the Christ, Lucifer), against the rulers of the darkness of this world, (Lucifer's principles are those of darkness, that subjects the human will, invoking the doctrines of force, in keeping with his original intent to destroy the agency of man), against spiritual wickedness in high places. (This latter, without doubt refers to the spiritual deception that will be forthcoming and was already at work within the church itself, causing it to sink into a state of rank apostasy.)[2]

---

[1] 2 Thess. 2.
[2] Eph. 6:11, 12.

Paul continues:

Wherefore (because of the above condition) take unto you the whole armour of God, that *ye* may be able to withstand in the *evil day,* and having done all, *to stand.*[3]

_____

[3]*Ibid.,* 6:13.

The Kingdom of Evil

It will be of interest to inquire into the functioning of the kingdom of evil. This kingdom, though normally unseen, is very real, as its un-embodied spirits, under the direction of Lucifer, the arch-enemy of Christ and all righteousness, wield a deceptive and wicked influence in the lives of men and women here upon the earth.

Forces of Evil Well-organized

Here in the ambient areas of the earth, to which Lucifer and his fallen angels were assigned when cast out from the pre-existent presence of God, a militant rebellion continues against God in opposing and attempting to frustrate the plan of salvation of which Jesus Christ is the author. It is important to regard it in this light to understand better the diabolical plan which these forces of evil have put into operation. With proper understanding and power, these evil influences that disseminate deceit and error can be detected and forestalled.

The Prophet Joseph Smith had many encounters with Lucifer himself, and there were unfolded to him by revelation and open vision, many details of his kingdom of evil, its power, laws, and government, concerning which he said,

> It is evident from the Apostles' writings, that many false spirits existed in their day, and had gone forth into the world, and that it needed intelligence which God alone could impart to detect false spirits, and to prove what spirits were of God. The world in general has been grossly ignorant in regard to this one thing, and why should they be otherwise—for no man knows the things of God, but by the Spirit of God.

> One great evil is, that men are ignorant of the nature of spirits; their power, laws, government, intelligence, etc., and imagine that when there is anything like power, revelation, or vision manifested, that it must be of God.[4]

---

[4]*Documentary History of the Church*, Vol. 4, p. 571.

It is to be noted from these remarks of the Prophet, that
the evil spirits are permitted to function within their own
realm and are often found to be demonstrating their powers
in the performance of what would be regarded as a miracle
to us mortals. Seeing the use of these powers, some are led
to believe that such is from God. For example, with regard
to the speaking in tongues, the Prophet in the same article
makes this statement:

> Again it may be asked, how it was that they could speak
> in tongues if they were of the devil! We would answer
> that they could be made to speak in another tongue, as
> well as their own, as they were under the control of that
> spirit, and the devil can tempt the Hottentot, the Turk, the
> Jew or any other nation; and if these men were under the
> influence of his spirit, they, of course, could speak Hebrew,
> Latin, Greek, Italian, Dutch or any other language that
> the devil knew.[5]

Evil Spirits Possess Former Knowledge

It is important to bear in mind, when contemplating
how the power of evil may affect our lives, that their
knowledge of the pre-existence of these evil spirits has
apparently not been taken from them. In possession of
this former knowledge and of us, they are in position to
wield an influence of evil, through our weaknesses. The
Prophet Joseph Smith has stated further:

> A man is saved no faster than he gets knowledge, for
> if he does not get knowledge, he will be brought into
> captivity by some evil power *in the other world,* as
> evil spirits will have more knowledge than many men
> who are on the earth. Hence it needs revelation to
> assist us (with the things taken from us because of the
> imposition of mortality), and give us knowledge of the
> things of God.[6]

Controlled by the Priesthood

There are many references in both ancient and modern scripture that reveal the presence of evil spirits in the

[5]*Idem.*
[6]*Ibid.*, Vol. 4, p. 588.

world. But these spirits, it is to be noted and fortunately for all, can be held in subjection, by revelation and the power of the priesthood. For by this power and delegated authority their mischievous and mysterious operations, when militated against the interests of the Church and the spread of truth in particular, are detected and can be controlled.

To indicate proper priesthood authority in dealing with evil spirits, consider the case of the seven sons of Sceva, vagabond Jews, exorcists, who took upon themselves the right to cast out evil spirits of him who was possessed, having witnessed the exercise of this power by Paul the apostle, and who then attempted to duplicate it by commanding the spirits to depart from the individual, in the name of the Lord Jesus whom Paul preached.

The evil spirits in the man, recognizing their lack of priesthood authority, replied,

Jesus I know, and Paul I know; but who are ye?[7]

Thereafter, as the biblical account records it, the evil spirits in the man leaped upon them so that they fled naked and wounded.

Evil Spirits Possess Bodies of Others

This incident, while establishing the need of the proper authority to deal with evil spirits, also makes known clearly the fact that evil spirits are actually prevalent in the earth and can, under certain circumstances, possess the bodies of others.

Another incident of noteworthy reference, giving some evidence of the number of evil spirits that roam the earth, concerns two maniacs who were sorely tormented by evil spirits, one of these at least, according to the Gospels, had been bound with fetters and chains, but, with demoniac power had broken them away and had fled to the mountains to live among the tombs like an animal. Night and

---

[7]Acts 19:15.

day his weird and terrifying shrieks could be heard. Seeing
Jesus, the poor creature ran toward and was prostrate before him, crying out with a loud voice,

> What have I to do with thee, Jesus, thou Son of the
> most high God?[8]

Jesus commanded the evil spirits to leave. One or
more of them, through the voice of the man, pleaded to
be left alone, and with blasphemous presumption ex-
claimed,

> I adjure thee by God, that thou torment me not—[8]
> Art thou come hither to torment us before the time?[9]

The demons, by whom the man was possessed and
controlled, recognized the Master, whom they knew they
had to obey; but they pleaded to be left alone until the
decreed time of their final punishment.

Legions of Spirits

Jesus asked, "What is thy name?" and the demons
within the man answered, "My name is Legion: for we
are many."[10] To get the full significance of this happening
one should study carefully the accounts recorded in Mat-
thew 8:28-34; Mark 5:1-19; Luke 8:26-39 and also James
E. Talmage, *Jesus the Christ*, pp. 310-311. (2000 swine)

These further incidents taken from the Holy Bible will
suffice to show that evil spirits do occupy the bodies and
minds of men, although there are many others that could
be referred to. This incident indicates how well the evil
spirits knew Jesus, and it is reasonable to assume that
they also know any who hold the priesthood and endeavor
to exercise its powers in behalf of the purposes of God.
This was also evident in the incident of the seven sons of
Sceva referred to, for well they knew the Apostle Paul, a
servant of God.

8Mark 5:7.
9Matthew 8:29.
10Mark 5:9.

Still another concerned Jesus while at Capernaum. There in the synagogue the Christ came face to face with a man who was possessed of an evil spirit. The Bible text states that he had, "a spirit of an unclean devil"; here, as upon other occasions, the man possessed of an evil spirit was terrified before our Lord and cried out with a loud voice,

> Let us alone; what have we to do with thee, thou Jesus of Nazareth? art thou come to destroy us? I know thee who thou art; the Holy One of God.[11]

Jesus rebuked the unclean spirits and commanded them to be silent, and leave the man, and they obeyed.

Upon still another occasion, the disciples were confronted with a lunatic who was possessed of an evil spirit, but they could not cast him out. Jesus, alarmed at their lack of faith in making the attempt to do so, chided them with a denunciation,

> O faithless and perverse generation, how long shall I be with you? how long shall I suffer you? bring him hither to me.[12]

Then Jesus rebuked the evil spirit, and he departed out of him; this chagrined the apostles who asked, "Why could not we cast him out?"

"Howbeit this kind," the Master replied, "goeth not out but by prayer and fasting."[13]

The Power of Evil in Our Day

Modern-day scriptures and experiences reveal many instances of a comparable nature to those of ancient times, indicating clearly that evil spirits do roam the earth today in our own time, to deceive and frustrate God's work as revealed unto the Prophet Joseph Smith.

> Verily, verily, I say unto you, that Satan has great

---

[11]Luke 4:33-34.
[12]Matthew 17:17.
[13]*Ibid.*, 17:19, 21.

hold upon their hearts; he stirreth them up to iniquity against that which is good;

And their hearts are corrupt, and full of wickedness and abominations; and they love darkness rather than light, because their deeds are evil; therefore they will not ask of me.

Satan stirreth them up, that he may lead their souls to destruction.

And thus he has laid a cunning plan, thinking to destroy the work of God; but I will require this at their hands, and it shall turn to their shame and condemnation in the day of judgment.

Yea, he stirreth up their hearts to anger against this work.

Yea, he saith unto them: Deceive and lie in wait to catch, that ye may destroy; behold, this is no harm. And thus he flattereth them, and telleth them that it is no sin to lie that they may catch a man in a lie, that they may destroy him. . . .

And thus he goeth up and down, to and fro in the earth, seeking to destroy the souls of men.[14]

Man Must Choose Revelation of God or of Lucifer

Brigham Young, who occupied the position of God's prophet following the martyrdom death of Joseph Smith, has spoken conclusively of the prevalence of evil spirits in the world and of their opposition to revelation from God. He further proclaims that the organization of the "Kingdom of Evil" is so established to attempt to match strides with the growth and development of the Church of the restoration in these latter days. Concerning this, and of the importance of accepting the revelations of God, he said,

It was revealed to me in the commencement of this Church, that the Church would spread, prosper, grow and extend, and that in proportion to the spread of the Gospel among the nations of the earth, so would the power of Satan rise. It was told you here that Brother Joseph warned the Elders of Israel against false spirits. It was revealed to me, *that if the people did not receive the spirit of revelation that God had sent for the salvation*

---

[14]D&C 10:20-27.

*of the world, they would receive false spirits and would
have their revelation*—It was not only revealed to Joseph
but to your humble servant, that false spirits would be
as prevalent and as common among the inhabitants of
the earth as we now see them.[15]

In the preface to the Doctrine and Covenants, a book
containing modern revelation, the Lord speaks unto his
servant the Prophet Joseph Smith of the dominion of the
devil and of how he will have power over his own.

For I am no respecter of persons, and will that all
men shall know that the day speedily cometh; the hour
is not yet, but is nigh at hand, when peace shall be taken
from the earth, *and the devil shall have power over his
own dominion.*[16]

This means, as explained by Brigham Young, that as
the Church expands its growth in the earth, Lucifer and
his kingdom of evil will become increasingly more active
in his own dominion, to restrain the forward movement of
the gospel plan revealed in this dispensation for the good
of man.

The Christ himself referred to Lucifer as the prince
of this world and indicates the extent of his evil power.[17]

Michael, the Archangel, Dispels Lucifer again

It is to be remembered that it was Michael, the archangel, who was called upon to expel Lucifer and his disobedient and rebellious, pre-existent followers from the
presence of God. The fact is that Michael, or Adam by
his human name, has the God-given assignment to keep
Lucifer within his bounds. Further evidence of this is seen
in the attempt made by Lucifer to thwart the bestowal of
the Melchizedek Priesthood, by Peter, James, and John
upon the heads of Joseph Smith and Oliver Cowdery.
Apparently, not having yet received the Higher Priesthood,
they were not able to detect the presence of Lucifer, who,

---

[15]*Discourses of Brigham Young*, pp. 110-111.
[16]D&C 1:35.
[17]John 12:31 and 14:30.

according to the words of the Prophet Joseph Smith, appeared on the Susquehanna River as an angel of light, to deceive them and no doubt to attempt to interfere with the conferring of the Holy Priesthood upon them. We are informed by the Prophet of the appearance there of Michael, the archangel, who came to detect the deception of Lucifer and banish him from the scene.

> The voice of Michael on the banks of the Susquehanna, detecting the devil when he appeared as an angel of light! The voice of Peter, James, and John in the wilderness between Harmony, Susquehanna county, and Colesville, Broome county, on the Susquehanna river, declaring themselves as possessing the keys of the kingdom, and of the dispensation of the fulness of times![18]

The demonstrated power of evil[19] against the Church has been constant since its establishment in these last days. A manifestation of how this evil force could weave its way into the very Church, reached its apex at Kirtland, Ohio, where the Prophet Joseph Smith was denounced by members and nonmembers alike, as a "fallen prophet." Some from within the Church had been his immediate friends and confidential advisers, and the divinity of his mission was being doubted by many who had only shortly before, received through him a testimony of the truth.

> "No quorum in the Church," says he, "was entirely exempt from the influence of those false spirits who were striving against me for the mastery. Even some of the Twelve were so far lost to their high and responsible calling, as to take sides, secretly, with the enemy.[20]

A Vivid Manifestation of Lucifer's Kingdom

No doubt one of the greatest demonstrations of the power of evil and the regimented forces of Lucifer against the Church, was experienced by our early missionaries to the British Isles. An account of this is taken from the *Journal of Heber C. Kimball*, who was present at the time.

----

[18]D&C 128:20.
[19]See Notes beginning p. 76 of this book.
[20]*Life of Heber C. Kimball*, p. 115.

It is interesting to note first that the Prophet Joseph Smith, who had set them apart to their missions, bestowed upon them the gift to "open the door of salvation to that nation."[21] Of the incident of the "kingdom of evil" we read,

> Sunday, July 30th, 1837, about daybreak, Elder Isaac Russell who slept with Elder Richards in Wilfred Street, came up to the third story, where Elder Hyde and myself were sleeping, and called out, "Brother Kimball, I want you to get up and pray for me that I may be delivered from the evil spirits that are tormenting me to such a degree, that I feel I cannot live long, unless I obtain relief."

> I had been sleeping on the back of the bed. I immediately arose, slipped off the foot of the bed, and passed around to where he was. Elder Hyde threw his feet out, and sat up in the bed, and we laid hands on him, I being mouth, and prayed that the Lord would have mercy on him, and rebuked the devil.

> While thus engaged I was struck with great force by some invisible power, and fell senseless to the floor. The first thing I recollected was being supported by Elders Hyde and Richards who then assisted me to get on the bed, but my agony was so great I could not endure it, and I arose, bowed my knees and prayed. I then arose and sat up on the bed, when a vision was opened to our minds, and we could distinctly see the evil spirits, who foamed and gnashed their teeth at us. We gazed upon them about an hour and a half (by Willard's watch). We were not looking toward the window but toward the wall. Space appeared before us, and we saw the devils coming in legions, with their leaders, who came within a few feet of us. They came toward us like armies rushing to battle. They appeared to be men of full stature, possessing every form and feature of men in the flesh, who were angry and desperate; and I shall never forget the vindictive malignity depicted on their countenances as they looked me in the eye; and any attempt to paint the scene which then presented itself, or portray their malice and enmity, would be vain—I felt excessive pain, and was in the greatest of distress for some time. I cannot even look back on the scene without feelings of horror; yet by it I learned the power of the adversary, his enmity against the servants of God, and we got some understanding of the invisible world. We

---

[21]See *History of the Church*, vol. II, pp. 489-90.

distinctly heard those spirits talk and express their
wrath, and hellish designs against us. However, the
Lord delivered us from them and blessed us exceedingly
that day.[22]

Elder Hyde also furnished a supplemental description
of the fearful scene described above, which corroborated
all that had been so stated by Heber C. Kimball.

Some time later, after the brethren had returned from
their mission in England, where great success had attended
their labors in that entire villages and congregations of
other churches were converted, and which was undoubtedly the cause of the demoniacal attack, Elder Kimball
narrated his experience to the Prophet Joseph Smith. He
asked the Prophet what it all meant, and whether there
was anything wrong with him, that he should have such a
manifestation. The answer given by the Prophet is most
enlightening and should be kept in mind by all who endeavor to serve the Lord in the building up of his kingdom
here upon the earth, wherein it is needful to be alert to
the powers of evil.

> "No, Brother Heber," said the Prophet, "at that time
> you were nigh unto the Lord; there was only a veil between
> you and Him, but you could not see Him. When I heard
> of it, (apparently the news of this encounter had come to
> the Prophet beforehand) it gave me great joy, for then I
> knew that the work of God had taken root in that land.
> It was this that caused the devil to make a struggle to
> kill you."[23]

The Prophet's Own Experience with Lucifer

How well the Prophet must have recalled at that time,
his own struggles with Lucifer, first, where as a young man
he had gone to seek guidance in the Sacred Grove when
an attempt was made to destroy him, to prevent the glorious vision from descending upon him which opened this
new dispensation; and of the many other encounters, in-

---

[22]Kimball, *op. cit.*, pp. 144-145; Preston—Ribble R.
[23]*Idem.*

cident to the coming forth of the Book of Mormon, and the divine bestowals involving the conferring of the keys for this dispensation. Yes, the Prophet above all other men upon the earth knew of the powers of Lucifer and his legions of unembodied spirits who fight day and night to frustrate the work of righteousness in the earth. These occurrences were not vague experiences, but actual encounters, for as he had told Heber C. Kimball, the closer we come to the Lord when the veil is thin, then the effort of Lucifer to deceive and mislead will be the greatest.

The Prophet related an experience to Heber C. Kimball that took place at Far West in a home which the Prophet had obtained for his family and which had formerly belonged to others who had used it as a public house or tavern. Heber C. Kimball recorded the story in his own journal. (This is no doubt the house which the Prophet and family occupied during the days of Far West and which stood just southeast from the temple site. This house in later years was visited by Andrew Jenson and also Brigham H. Roberts, Church Historians, as contained in their historical accounts, and which stood on the ground where now stands a small Reorganized LDS Chapel— 1961.)

> A short time after he got into it, one of his children was taken very sick; he laid his hands on the child's head; when it got better, as soon as he went out-of-doors, the child was taken sick again; he again laid his hands upon it, so that it again recovered. This occurred several times, when Joseph inquired of the Lord, what it all meant; then he had an open vision, and saw the devil in person, who contended with Joseph face to face for some time. He said it was his house, it belonged to him, and Joseph had no right to be there. Then Joseph rebuked Satan in the name of the Lord, and he departed and touched the child no more.[24]

Lucifer Seeks after the More Righteous

After these presumed reflections the Prophet Joseph

---

[24]*Ibid.*, p. 270.

Smith continued his interview with Heber C. Kimball, concerning their adventure in Preston, England, with the forces of the domain of evil, for said he,

> The nearer a person approaches the Lord, a greater power will be manifested by the adversary to prevent the accomplishment of His purposes.[25]

There can be no question that in the ushering in of all great gospel dispensations, wherein divine messengers are sent from the presence of God, in resuscitating by bestowal the various keys and priesthood authority needed for the functioning of the gospel of Jesus Christ upon the earth, Lucifer has tried in every way at his command to prevent the chosen servants of God here upon the earth from receiving these gifts and powers.[26] Lucifer knows well his ultimate doom and confinement.[27] Still he continues his efforts, not having been decisively beaten, when he and his angels were expelled from the presence of God in the pre-existence, hoping still to gather sufficient strength to overcome eventually the forces of righteousness. In this, of course, he will fail, for his lot is cast, and with him all who follow after him, for theirs is an eternal doom to be confined in that place prepared for them, not a place of glory, but a place of darkness.

NOTES

> Who hath appointed Michael your prince, and established his feet, and set him upon high, and given unto him the keys of salvation under the counsel and direction of the Holy One, who is without beginning of days or end of life.[28]

Michael, or Adam as he is known by his name here in mortality, was an associate in the creation of this earth and thus held a high and noble position in the pre-existent realm. This is further indicated by the fact that it was he who directed the checking and expulsion of Lucifer in his

---

[25]*Ibid.*, pp. 145-146.
[26]See Notes on this page.
[27]Rev. 12.
[28]D&C 78:16.

pre-existent effort to gain ascendancy above the council of
Gods because of his proposed plan involving the doctrine
of force and the forfeiture of agency, which he attempted
to place in operation for the earth life existence of man.

The priesthood after the order of the Son of God, as
it was known in the pre-existence, known here upon the
earth as the Melchizedek, contains the power that will con-
tain Lucifer within the bounds of his habitation, and eventually, after the plan of this life is completed will place
him with those who are his followers, both from the pre-
existent period, and also during the period of mortality, in
that sphere or kingdom which has been prepared for him.
They rejected the priesthood of God, and they in their
fallen state, devoid of any capability to repent, seek now,
as then, to change the plan of life and salvation, as it is
now in effect upon the earth.

Theirs is a forlorn cause, but until Lucifer and his
kingdom of evil are fully subjected, which in due time will
be their fate, he continues his harassment of the work of
the Lord. But the Lord cannot permit Lucifer to interfere
in key situations where the establishment of the gospel and
the exercise of agency can be implanted in the lives of those
upon the earth. The calling of Michael, the great prince,
in controlling the activities of Lucifer in his role as the
leader of the opposition of evil in the earth life of man is
clearly seen by references to key scriptures.

1. Leadership of the pre-existent forces that cast
Satan and his followers from the presence of God.

> And there was war in heaven: Michael and his angels
> fought against the dragon; and the dragon fought and
> his angels,
>
> And prevailed not; neither was their place found
> any more in heaven.
>
> And the great dragon was cast out, that old serpent,
> called the Devil, and Satan, which deceiveth the whole
> world: he was cast out into the earth, and his angels were
> cast out with him.[29]

---

[29]Rev. 12:7-9.

2. The attempt made by Lucifer to take the body of Moses frustrated by Michael.

> Yet Michael the archangel, when contending with the devil he disputed about the body of Moses, durst not bring against him a railing accusation, but said, the Lord rebuke thee.[30] (Here Lucifer is permitted to continue but not to the extent of the destruction of Moses, wherein a key gospel situation was at stake.)

3. The detecting and dispelling of Lucifer on the banks of the Susquehanna River at the time of the conferment of the Melchizedek Priesthood by Peter, James, and John.

> The voice of Michael on the banks of the Susquehanna, detecting the devil when he appeared as an angel of light! The voice of Peter, James and John in the wilderness between Harmony, Susquehanna county, and Colesville, Broome county, on the Susquehanna river, declaring themselves as possessing the keys of the kingdom, and of the dispensation of the fulness of times![31]

4. At the conclusion of the earth life plan of man, Michael will be the great general of the righteous forces that will subdue and bind Satan forever.

> And Michael, the seventh angel, even the archangel, shall gather together his armies, even the hosts of heaven.
>
> And the devil shall gather together his armies; even the hosts of hell, and shall come up to battle against Michael and his armies.
>
> And then cometh the battle of the great God; and the devil and his armies shall be cast away into their own place, that they shall not have power over the saints any more at all.
>
> For Michael shall fight their battles, and shall overcome him who seeketh the throne of him who sitteth upon the throne, even the Lamb.[32]

Reference is made to other attempts made by Lucifer to prevent the work of God from going forward.

---

[30]Jude 9; P. of G. P., Moses ch. 1.
[31]D&C 128:20.
[32]*Ibid.*, 88:112-115; 76:31-48.

1. The deceiving of the children of Adam. The beginning of the sons of men.[33] The oath of unrighteous dominion. The secret of Mahan. The killing of Abel by Cain to obtain the birthright of Abel.

2. The vision of Enoch and the power of Satan over mankind.

3. The attempt made to deceive Moses as he approached the Sinai appointment with God and his Son Jesus Christ.[34]

4. The temptation of Christ by Lucifer, and his acknowledgment that Lucifer was temporarily the god of this world.

> All these things will I give thee, if thou wilt fall down and worship me.[35]

5. The incident in the Sacred Grove. The menace of evil in the destruction of Joseph Smith by the presence and destructive force of Lucifer, prevented by the appearance of God the Father and his Son Jesus Christ.[36]

The Beginning of Evil in the Earth

The question may properly be asked, how did Lucifer and his disciples of deceit come to be upon the earth, to menace the plan of salvation, to harass mankind, and to oppose righteousness?

An account of the expulsion of Lucifer and his angels from the presence of God in the pre-existence is told in the manifestations to the Apostle John, the beloved of the Lord. He was given the promise of continuous life in the flesh until the second coming of Jesus Christ. Yet because of the preaching of the gospel of Christ he was banished to the Isle of Patmos, by order of Domitian the emperor

---

[33]A designation given to those in early times who did not subscribe to the commandments and teachings of righteousness. Those who did subscribe were referred to as the sons and daughters of God. (See Gen. 6:2; P. of G. P., Moses 7:1; 8:14, 15.)

[34]See page 83.

[35]Matthew 4:9; John 14:30.

[36]Joseph Smith's Own Story.

of Rome in the year 96 A.D. While there he was privileged
to see in open vision and manifestation, a panoramic view
of the prophesied happenings of this earth and her people
from the beginning to the end. Part of the vision reached
back into the pre-existent sphere of man, where events
pertaining to Lucifer and his effort to gain power were
clearly seen. These are the words of the Apostle John, as
he related the fall of Satan:

> And there was war in heaven: Michael and his angels
> fought against the dragon; and the dragon fought and
> his angels,
> And prevailed not; neither was their place found any
> more in heaven.
> And the great dragon was cast out, that old serpent,
> called the Devil, and Satan, which deceiveth the whole
> world: he was cast out *into the earth*, and his angels were
> cast out with him.[37]

In recording the events of the same vision, verse four
of the same chapter, John indicates that so powerful was
the influence of Lucifer at that time, he drew like kind as
himself,

> . . . the third part of the stars of heaven. . . .[38]

These under the direction of Lucifer not only rejected
the commandments but also opposed God and the forces
of righteousness; they also extended their diabolical plan
in accusations against some of the noble leaders or "brethren" day and night.

Thus the Apostle John witnessed the dispute in heaven
which arrayed the forces of Lucifer against the forces of
God, ending in the expulsion of Lucifer and his hosts from
the presence of God. The conditions of this dispute have
been made known in clearness to the Prophet Joseph
Smith. From the Book of Moses,

> And I, the Lord God, spake unto Moses, saying:
> That Satan, whom thou hast commanded in the name of

---

[37]Rev. 12:7-9.
[38]*Ibid.*, 12:4.

mine Only Begotten, is the same which was from the beginning, and he came before me, saying—Behold, here am I, send me, I will be thy son, and I will redeem all mankind, that one soul shall not be lost, and surely I will do it; wherefore give me thine honor.[39]

This statement was made to Moses because of the encounter he had just experienced with Lucifer, wherein he had attempted to deceive him into believing that he, Lucifer, was the god of the earth and had instructed him, to come and worship him—God therefore is identifying Lucifer unto Moses. We continue to read from the account given above,

But, behold, my Beloved Son, which was my Beloved and Chosen from the beginning, said unto me—Father, thy will be done, and the glory be thine forever.[40]

We are told in this that Christ sought nothing for himself in the way of glory. He proposed no plan contrary to the God-given plan, only the desire to do the will of the Father, in preserving the right of agency.

Lucifer and his followers could not subscribe to this plan, because in its personal salvation phase, it required that *repentance* be exercised, to bring about a personal change, a new birth. And repentance as an action, requires the unqualified exercise of agency—for man to know the difference between good and evil, and then by right of agency, choose the good, is the crowning achievement of man when pursued to attain personal salvation. Lucifer and his followers had lost the power to repent, hence they opposed God's plan.

Continuing, God said unto Moses,

Wherefore, because that Satan rebelled against me, *and sought to destroy the agency of man, which I*, the Lord God, had given him, and also, that I should give unto him mine own power; by the power of mine Only Begotten, I caused that he should be cast down.

[39]Moses 4:1.
[40]*Ibid.*, 4:2.

And he became Satan, yea, even the devil, the father
of all lies, to deceive and to blind men, and to lead them
captive at his will, even as many as would not hearken
unto my voice.[41]

Note: The expulsion of Lucifer and those who followed him from the
pre-existent sphere, was obviously done, because they no longer could be a
part of the plan of earth life, or second estate of man, which was at that
time in its final stage of launching. There was no reason for them to remain
there, and since their ultimate abode, "the kingdom of darkness," is being
prepared for them, and which they will ultimately occupy, they were cast
down upon the earth, the only apparent place they could be sent, and which,
being known beforehand by God, became another factor to deal with in the
progress of the spirit children of God.

Effects of Lucifer's Plan Seen

The concept of life which Lucifer sought to impose
upon the children of God, would take from them the right
to choose between good and evil. Their eventual salvation,
under his plan, would be a matter of compulsion. *Faith*,
the prime requisite of life upon the earth, would not be a
part of the plan of salvation, and the whole course of life
would be one of the rankest predestination, with all things
completely decided beforehand, thus eliminating the need
of a probation where the children of God could prove, unto
God and themselves, by an obtained worthiness, their fit-
ness for the spheres of glory in the life to follow this one,
which provides that man shall find his place in that sphere
best suited to his limitations and aspirations, and to that
degree of obedience to righteous law that he can attain.

Under the plan of Lucifer, man would become nothing
but a serf, something to be acted upon only and not to act.
In time, as is wisely seen by our Heavenly Father, and the
other noble ones, if such a course were pursued, retrogression would set in, and the nobility of man would
change to that of a lower order. Of this we know little
except that it would be a place of darkness.

So far was the concept of Lucifer wrong and contrary
to the purpose of righteousness, that the necessity of an
open warfare, in the pre-existent realms was risked and
encountered, to preserve the *rights of agency*, so necessary
to the salvation and eternal joy of man.

---

[41]*Ibid.*, 4:3-4.

The power of Lucifer in this encounter is seen in the fact, as revealed to the Apostle John, that one-third of the hosts of heaven, believed and were susceptible to deception by him, and in following him in open rebellion, became like unto him, incapable of repentance and committed to the purpose of continuing their opposition as long as they are permitted to do so. Since the struggle of these two forces was not settled in the pre-existence, notwithstanding the fact that he and his angels were cast out of the presence of God, they are permitted to abide in the ambient area of the earth, and in such position continue their efforts to deceive and influence the embodied sons and daughters of God from their search for and obedience to the laws of righteousness to achieve placement in the degrees of glory which God has ordained for his children.

Just how well Lucifer has succeeded in his plan, can easily be seen by the following references. It is to be remembered, however, that unless those who have been embodied sin against the Holy Ghost, Satan will eventually have no power over them. His intention, therefore, is to relegate mankind to the lowest depth possible. In this respect, the Apostle John tells of his power and method:

> . . . *Satan, which deceiveth the whole world.*[42]

When men are deceived, they can be subjected to systems or rule of governments which exercise powers of unrighteous dominion that does not allow in those that are governed, the rights of *agency*.

The Coming of Priestcraft

The Establishment of Priestcraft with Covenants and Oaths of Secrecy—to Oppose the Rights and Functions of the Priesthood of God.

Moses relates the action of Lucifer, as he pursued his own plan, unto the early inhabitants of the earth.

---

[42]Rev. 12:9.

> And Satan came among them, (family of Adam and
> Eve) saying: I am also a son of God (and some believed
> him), . . . and they loved Satan more than God. And men
> began from that time forth to be carnal, sensual, and
> devilish.[43]

> And Cain loved Satan more than God. And Satan
> commanded him, saying: Make an offering unto the
> Lord.[44]

But this offering, so advocated by Lucifer, was not in
accordance with the commandments of God and, therefore, was a deception. The Lord God, detecting this, told
Cain that he could still be saved from Lucifer if he would
hearken to his words, but if he would not, that notwithstanding he would rule over Satan, (because of a resurrected body) he nevertheless, would become the father of
all lies to the children of men, and he himself perdition,
because of the initiation of these principles unto the children of men upon the earth.

Cain continued to follow Satan and covenanted with
him to establish more firmly these doctrines upon the
earth. This was all done through the principles of priestcraft, involving unrighteous dominion over the lives of
men, which constitutes the very plan which he had advocated in the pre-existent conflict. Here then, upon the
earth, was the introduction of the very forces of evil which
Lucifer would have imposed openly upon all of us in a
plan of life, had he not been restrained in the pre-existence.
Despite all this, it remains, in the providence of God, that
Lucifer is permitted to function within his realm here
upon the earth.

The Need of Opposition

Thus, in the wisdom of God, was established, by the
very application of agency itself, one form of opposition,
which will ever be necessary in the plan of the gospel.
In describing the need of opposition in all things, Lehi also

---

[43]P. of G. P., Moses 5:13.
[44]Ibid., 5:18.

points out the manner of living to which we all would be submitted if there was not an opposition in all things.

> For it must needs be, that there is an opposition in all things. If not so, my first-born in the wilderness, righteousness could not be brought to pass, neither wickedness, neither holiness nor misery, neither good nor bad. Wherefore, all things must needs be a compound in one; wherefore, if it should be one body it must needs remain as dead, having no life neither death, nor corruption nor incorruption, happiness nor misery, neither sense nor insensibility.[45]

Satan himself, knowing well the plan of God in this regard, has set up an opposition to God's will in the plan of life and salvation. Wishfully thinking, for he knows of his eventual doom, but that he might, through the weakness of the flesh of men, gain sufficient additional following, he pursues his lost cause, born out of a grim reality that he can do no other, for this is the type of being he is. But he deceives even himself as he hopes to defeat the purposes of God. But God, not fearful of this and knowing full well of the eventual triumph, permits Satan to remain within the ambient area of the earth, operating within his own unembodied kingdom of evil to serve the over-all purposes of the plan of life.

An evidence that he is to be permitted to continue in this manner is indicated by the statement of the Prophet Joseph Smith,

> The spirits of good men cannot interfere with the wicked beyond their prescribed bounds, for Michael, the archangel, dared not bring a railing accusation against the devil, but said, "The Lord rebuke thee, Satan."[46]

Lucifer, a Prince of the Power of the Air

From the further writings of the Prophet Joseph Smith, we learn of some of the characteristics of those of the kingdom of evil and of certain traits of power which Lucifer himself possesses.

------
[45] 2 Nephi 2:11.
[46] *Teachings of the Prophet Joseph Smith*, (Joseph Fielding Smith) p. 208.

It would seem also, that wicked spirits have their
bounds, limits, and laws by which they are governed or
controlled, and know their future destiny; hence, those
that were in the maniac said to our Savior, "Art thou
come to torment us before the time,"—and when Satan
presented himself before the Lord, among the sons of
God, he said that he came "from going to and fro in the
earth, and from wandering up and down in it"; *and he
is emphatically called the prince of the power of the air;*
and, it is very evident that they possess a power that none
but those who have the Priesthood can control.[47]

Satan, therefore, to oppose the priesthood, established among the children of Adam in the beginning, the
principles of priestcraft. This condition is described
further by Moses,

And Satan said unto Cain: Swear unto me by thy
throat, and if thou tell it thou shalt die; and swear thy
brethren by their heads, and by the living God, that
they tell it not; for if they tell it they shall surely die; and
this that thy father may not know it; and his day I will
deliver thy brother Abel into thine hands.[48]

The establishing of priestcraft with its covenants and
oaths, was not done for the sole purpose of perpetrating
the murder of Abel, but to mislead and deceive the sons
and daughters of Adam, so that in the deception and following the course which Satan had put before them, they
would deny unto themselves the priesthood of God, which
Lucifer knew well was the source of power that could
detect his deceptions and dispel him as was needed to
further the work of our Heavenly Father. But Cain was
decived by Lucifer in believing that with Abel out of the
way, he would receive the birthright, and inherit the riches
of his father Adam's house, even without the priesthood
birthright.

Lucifer Held Great Power over Sons of Adam

The extent of the power of Lucifer over Cain and other

---

[47]*Documentary History of the Church,* Vol. 4; Eph. 2:2; John 12:31, 14:30
(Prince of air—Lucifer prince of this world to come after death of Jesus.)
[48]P. of G. P., Moses 5:29.

children of Adam can be learned from the further writings of Moses.

> And Satan sware unto Cain that he would do accord-
> to his commands. And all these things were done in
> secret.
>
> And Cain said: Truly I am Mahan, the master of this
> great secret, that I may murder and get gain. Wherefore
> Cain was called Master Mahan, *and he gloried in his
> wickedness.*[49]

The effects of establishing these corrupt principles of priestcraft, are seen in the fact, that it was not long thereafter, that those who had followed Cain were insatiated with the lust for power and the exercising of unjust principles of government over others, thereby attempting to deny the rights of free agency, which God had decreed should be the right of all. This unrighteous dominion over others, when forces of evil are at work as has proved so down through the periods of history, leads directly to the destruction of those who will not obey the mandates of those who hold power. Witness in these further writings of Moses, concerning the tragic developments of early times, the exact initial pattern of what we have seen and been informed on, in every period of history, including our own present day, the operation of these unjust forces of evil, as they impose upon all under them, the principles of unrighteous dominion, which are in very essence the principles of priestcraft.

> For Lamech having entered into a covenant with
> Satan, (Lamech was the fiifth generation from Adam—
> Enoch—Irad—Mahujael—Methusael—Lamech); after the
> manner of Cain, wherein he became Master Mahan, master
> of that great secret which was administered unto Cain by
> Satan; and Irad, the son of Enoch, having known their
> secret, began to reveal it unto the sons of Adam; where-
> fore Lamech, being angry, slew him, (his great-grand-
> father) not like unto Cain, his brother Abel, for the sake of
> getting gain, but he slew him for the oath's sake.

------

[49]P. of G. P., Moses 5:30-31.

For, from the days of Cain, there was a secret combination, and their works were in the dark, *and they knew
every man his brother.*

Wherefore the Lord cursed Lamech, and his house,
and all them that had covenanted with Satan; for they
kept not the commandments of God, and it displeased
God, and he ministered not unto them, and their works
were abominations, and began to spread among all the
sons of men.[50]

The Founding of Unrighteous Governments

Thus, this unholy and unrighteous form of government
established in the beginning of man's occupancy of the
earth, has had its influence upon mankind almost con-
sistently and without exception, (Enoch and his city—The
children of Nephi for a period) down through the stream
of time. The coming of the flood in the days of Noah
but restrained and retarded it, and while preventing it
from destroying the plan of God and taking over completely, it, nevertheless, has persisted since the days of
the flood in much the same manner. The wisdom of God,
however, keeps it under check now with the placing upon
the earth of the priesthood of God.

History Records the Tool of Lucifer in Corrupt Government

Students of history can trace the functioning of this
power of evil in the earth, where through governments,
there is constantly the exercised power of unrighteous
dominion over the masses. The subjugation of their will,
the non-recognition of God-given rights, the wanton destruction of people in mass murders, simulating in greater
fashion even, the once secret covenants of Mahan. Consider the mighty kingdom of Nimrod, with its millions of
slave labor, or the onward slaughtering forces of the great
warrior Alexander, knowing no creed but the creed of
power and force. People meant nothing to these one-time
world governments. Other instances could be cited from
ancient times to show the preservation of the pattern of the

---

[50]P. of G. P., Moses 5:49-52.

pattern of unjust dominion, which Lucifer gave to the sons
of Adam.   His effort and purpose being, to frustrate the
plan of God, and if possible, to defeat the plan of *righteous
dominion,* and of the agency of man.

Other Great World Powers of Evil

The story of the seven great monarchies of antiquity,
the Chaldaean, the Assyrian, the Medean, the Babylonian,
the Persian, the Parthian, and the Sassanian or New Persian empires, is one of continuing lust for power, and of
aggression.   All of them exhibited that kind of covetous-
ness which we always find in those who seek to exercise
unrighteous dominion over their fellow men.

Not being content with the possessions and the power
they already claimed their own, they invaded the territories
of neighboring countries, with the object of subjugating
them.   To find that they met with success in any of their
aggressive undertakings only served to create a desire
for more power.   These ancient powers always kept
a watchful eye on their neighbors.   If these showed any
sign of weakness, or gave any other evidence of being an
easy prey, they would fall on them, in the exercise of the
doubtful right of the stronger.   And they would march on
until they met with some power which was able to check
their onslaught.

It began right with the first monarchy, the Chaldaeans.
Nimrod, the founder of this kingdom, "the mighty hunter"
of the scriptures, spread his kingdom inland, subduing or
expelling the various tribes which occupied the territory
in doing so.   His rule was so oppressive that Abraham was
forced to quit the country.

The Assyrians became "worthy" successors of the
Chaldaeans.   They made annual inroads into the territories of their neighbors.   They would overturn, beat to
pieces, and consume with fire the towns, sweep the country
with their troops, and impress upon the inhabitants the
fear of their presence.   The ferocity of their wars was such

that for every head of a foeman brought back to camp, the Assyrian soldiers received a reward.

Vanity played a great part, too. Tiglath-Pileser I, one of the most powerful Assyrian monarchs, who claims to have conquered forty-two countries in the course of but five campaigns, glories in his power, and calls himself, "the powerful king of the people of various tongues; king of the four regions; king of all kings; lord of lords; the supreme; monarch of monarchs; the illustrious chief . . . the conqueror of many plains and mountains of the upper and lower country; the victorious hero, the terror of whose name has overwhelmed all regions."

War is always an evil, but the wars of these monarchies were accompanied by inhuman atrocities. The complete disregard for the individual is seen as the inhabitants of captured places were treated with inhuman severity. Under the Assyrians, the leaders of the resistance received one of the usual modes of punishment: impalement, beating in their skull with a mace, flaying with a knife (sometimes even when still alive), or mutilation (by cutting off their ears or noses, by blinding them, or by plucking out their tongues by the roots). Many of the others were sentenced into slavery.

Asshur-bani-pal, one of the later Assyrian kings, was especially evil in this regard. He not only gave orders for the most barbarous cruelties to be performed, but even had them represented in all their horrors upon his palace walls.

The Medes were wont to commit the worst outrages. They would not only "dash to pieces" the fighting men of the nations opposed to them, allowing no quarter, but inflict indignities and cruelties on the women and children, which the pen unwillingly records. Infants were slain before the eyes of the parent, and the women ravished in the most brutal manner. They had no interest in spoil, they lusted for blood, the shedding of it, and the destroying of human life. The Babylonians mutilated their prisoners, massacred non-combatants, and they too executed the children before the eyes of the parents.

One of the problems of these conquerors was to keep the subjugated countries under effective control and to discourage their rebellion from the heavy yoke placed upon them. Various measures were taken to accomplish this. It was the custom for these monarchies to take recourse to wholesale deportation. Sargon, who removed the Israelites from Samaria to other parts of the empire, employed these measures on an especially grand scale. The object was to weaken the stronger races by dispersion, and to destroy the patriotic spirit of the weaker nations. These people were either settled in other parts of the empire, or they were employed as forced laborers.

Sargon, the Assyrian, established fortified posts in the various countries of his empire, and placed in them a great standing army, to stand on guard and keep the inhabitants in check. The Medes claimed suzerainty only over the nations immediately upon their borders; the remoter tribes they placed under these nations, and looked to them to collect and remit the tribute of the outlying countries. Darius, the Persian, organized his empire into satrapies, with a satrap over them who was liable to be recalled or put to death on the merest whim of the monarch. But while in power, these satraps ruled as despotically as they could.

In spite of all these measures, rebellion against the heavy yoke of the master was seething almost everywhere, and the monarch never hesitated to deal with such rebellions with the utmost force and brutality he had at his command. Under the Persians, crucifixion or impalement of some sort was the ordinary punishment for rebellion. According to Herodotus, 3,000 Babylonians were crucified by order of Darius to punish their revolt from him.

These severe measures were not only taken against the people of other nations, the same despotic power was also exercised over the monarch's own people. The Medes, for instance, did not hesitate to place some special troops

in the rear of their armies to kill every soldier who had not
the mind to attack the enemy.

In Persia, as in other empires, the monarch was the
state. He ruled as an absolute despot. The power of the
king was unlimited. He was the lord and master of the
people, the absolute disposer of their lives, liberties, and
property; the sole fountain of law and right, incapable
himself of doing wrong, one whose favor was happiness,
at whose frown men trembled, before whom all bowed
themselves down with the lowest and humblest obeisance.
Prostration—the attitude of worship—was required of all as
they entered the presence of the king. As a result, tyranny
was allowed to rule unchecked in the wildest caprices
and extravagances.

Any one of the subjects, even the highest nobles, would
be heavily punished if he incurred by a slight fault the
displeasure of the monarch. In Babylon, cutting to pieces
and casting into a heated furnace were among the recognized punishments. The houses of the offenders were
pulled down and made into dunghills. In Persia, the nobles
were liable to be beheaded, to be stoned to death, to be
suffocated with ashes, to have their tongues torn out by
the roots, to be buried alive, to be shot in mere wantonness,
to be flayed and then crucified, to be buried all but the
head, and to perish by the lingering agony of "the boat."
Their wives and daughters might be seized and horribly
mutilated, or buried alive, or cut into a number of fragments. It was the element of force—brutal force—that
held these empires together.

But as always in a totalitarian state, the powerful man
himself fears for his life and station. And sometimes there
is an internal struggle for power in the royal family. This
we find in the Parthian kingdom. Here the jealousy and
apprehensiveness went to such a head that the king had all
his male relatives murdered, for fear they might claim the
throne. The brother murdered his brother, and the son
murdered his father.

Many of these monarchs were great builders. The problem of obtaining the necessary laborers they easily solved. They put to work captives taken in war, or rebels from other parts of the empire. These forced laborers were placed under taskmasters who urged them on with blows. Often these unfortunates were forced to work in fetters.

There was no freedom, not even religious freedom. Nebuchadnezzar, for instance, changed his religion several times, and in every case he forced all of his subjects to embrace the same religion. During several periods in the course of these monarchies, the priests were given great powers. They were made wealthy by the offerings of the faithful and, as they held influential positions in the civil government, they were feared by the people.

When Artaxerxes founded the Sassanian or New Persian empire, he felt that the altar and the throne had to be inseparable. He raised the Magian priesthood to the great council of the nation, and enforced their decisions by pains and penalties. By an edict of Artaxerxes, all places of worship were closed but those of the Zoroastrians. The Magians took advantage of their position, and under various monarchs, and at various times, Christianity as well as other religious was cruelly persecuted and its adherents massacred, one of the worst persecutions having been that under Varahran I (272-275 A.D.).[51]

Nor should we pass hurriedly over ancient Babylonia, with its capital of Babylon located on the Euphrates River about seventy miles south of the present Baghdad. This wicked civilization flourished, with its ill-conceived principles of unrighteous dominion, 2500 years before Christ, continuing, until overthrown by the Assyrian armies under King Sennacherib, about 700 years B.C. A century later this mighty but still wicked kingdom was overthrown by the Chaldeans.

The fall of Nineveh, the capital of this kingdom, brought forth this declaration from the Prophet Nahum,

---

[51]Notes taken from Rawlinson *The Seven Great Monarchies.*

... all that hear the bruit of thee shall clap the hands
over thee: for upon whom hath not thy wickedness passed
continually?[52]

Nineveh was steeped in priestcraft and wickedness;
before her destruction, against this wickedness and power
of evil the Prophet Nahum fearlessly continued his procla-
mation of the wrath of God.

Woe to the bloody city! it is all full of lies (deception)
and robbery. . . .

The horseman lifteth up both the bright sword and
the glittering spear: and there is a multitude of slain, and
a great number of carcasses; and there is none end of their
corpses; they stumble upon their corpses:

Because of the multitude of the whoredoms of the
wellfavoured harlot, the mistress of witchcrafts, *that
selleth nations* through her whoredoms, and families
through her witchcrafts.

Behold, I am against thee, saith the Lord of hosts;
and I will discover thy skirts upon thy face, and I will
shew the nations thy nakedness, and the kingdoms thy
shame.[53]

The fall of Nineveh, however, did not end the channels of evil government through which Satan could carry
on his plan of the destruction of the agency of man, for
in this manner he sought to make it impossible for man
in any way to benefit from the obedient and voluntary plan
of the gospel of Christ.

Nebuchadnezzar, perhaps the greatest of all Chaldean
emperors, gave rise to another great citadel of crime and
deception, and became so mighty as to rule most of the
ancient world. This is the government of *unrighteous
dominion* that carried the Jews into captivity in 587 B.C.

Lucifer and His Own Destruction

But the devil has a way of destroying his own. For
the principles which he inculcates cannot long survive in
the government of men. Its very doctrine is one of decay

---

[52]Nahum 3:19.
[53]*Ibid.*, 3:1-5.

and dissolution. Its survival, if but for the brief span of intermittence in mortal life, depends upon a re-bestowal of deception and error upon the duped minds of those who themselves are cursed with the inclinations of evil, and who, because of their own evil tendencies are lifted up in high places, to administer the doctrines and teachings of Lucifer and his unseen band upon the innocent and wicked subjects alike who happen to fall under their dominion.

And so, this second Babylon was destroyed by its own lust for unjust power, felled by the rising force of the Medes and Persians in 538 B.C.

Notes

See Job 2:1, 2 and Job 1:7—Satan had apparently been on the earth before he presented his plan and was rejected.

Comment: Rev. 12:9—Witnesses—the casting out of Satan so he could not have come before God afterward. See also D&C 76:25.

Also—See D&C 29:36, 37. Lucifer was upon the earth before Adam. He had also been upon the earth before his expulsion from heaven. See DHC Vol. 4.

The Founding of Priestcraft to Meet the Birth of Christ

Following these times came the return of the Jews to Palestine, and perhaps the establishment of a worse priestcraft than those which had gone before, and which had so wantonly exercised the principles of Mahan in the slaughter of its subjects. Lucifer well knew that the time was approaching for the coming of the Son of Man, the Christ, the Only Begotten of the Father—the Redeemer of the world.

Under the leadership of Ezra and Nehemiah, two valiant men of God, a strong attempt was made to establish once again the house of Israel, at least that part of it upon the earth left to be established. This constituted principally the descendants of Judah. But here, as before, Lucifer pursued his evil purposes, and caused to be integrated into this new movement the priestly order of the Pharisees, under whom, with the guise of saintly purity, the leadership of the Jews was poisoned with a deception far more deadly, if it were possible, than that which had been manifest among the pagans.

The Priestcraft of Meridian Days

The Pharisee felt himself above others and promoted the idea of a priestly caste, encouraging self-sufficiency and spiritual pride. The Pharisees could have done much to have prepared the way for the coming of Christ into mortality, but actuated by the power of Lucifer, became instead a *priestcraft*, such a one, as declared by the Prophet Jacob, which would bring about the crucifixion of their God.

> Wherefore, as I said unto you, it must needs be expedient that Christ . . . should come among the Jews, among those who are the more wicked part of the world; and they shall crucify him—for thus it behooveth our God, and there is none other nation on earth, (deceived and led by their priestcraft leaders, the Pharisees), that would crucify their God.
>
> But because of priestcrafts and iniquities, they at Jerusalem will stiffen their necks against him, *that he be crucified.*[54]

Lucifer Establishes a Deceptive Temple of God

Following the death of Christ and his apostles, with the exception of John the beloved, there arose in the earth a kingdom of unrighteous dominion, so powerful, so dominant, as to place a pall of darkness upon the entire earth, producing what is commonly known as the "dark ages." At no time in the world's history has there been a period of time when the suppression of human rights has been more in evidence. That this should be at a time when a supposed Christian church was upon the earth indicates the extent of Satan's power over his own dominion in governments of men or in religious dynasties that would take unto themselves the power of directing, not only the affairs of men that go to constitute his everyday living, but also his religious thought. Herein is *an invasion of God's house.*

---

[54] 2 Nephi 10:3, 5.

and it sounds a warning that the tentacles of the power of evil can find their way into any church, institution, or kingdom that departs from the true ways of the Living God.

The Apostasy Directed by Lucifer Known in Advance by the Apostles of Christ

This particular kingdom of evil, which established itself in the would-be very Church of Christ, through a vast "falling away" from the original teachings of the Christ and his apostles, is perhaps seen best in the eyes of vision, given unto the Apostle Paul, who sensed, while yet living, the impending disaster that would befall the Christian church, which he and the other apostles labored to crystallize following the death of their Beloved Master. The other apostles saw this condition, too, for had not Lucifer succeeded, through priestcraft, in having his enemy, the Only Begotten of the Father, crucified, only, of course, as Jesus would permit him to do so? Lucifer could not control him, though hard he tried in the temptation of Christ, so he schemed to have him killed, that he might get on with the temporary destruction of his teachings and philosophy of life comprising the plan of salvation. What better time, must he have thought, to restrain the forces of good and the projection of truth, than at this time, as it had fallen from the very lips of Christ himself?

So Lucifer exerted great force and power and succeeded in establishing a kingdom of darkness and oppression, aptly described by Paul,

> Let no man deceive you by any means: for that day shall not come, (that day meaning the second coming of Christ which some had erroneously put into the minds of the saints at Thessalonica, and which impression the Apostle Paul was now correcting), except there come a *falling away first*, and that man of sin be revealed, the son of perdition;
>
> Who opposeth and exalteth himself above all that is called God, or that is worshipped (here we see the pattern of the attempted kingdom of evil which Lucifer would set up in opposition to the kingdom of God); so that he

as God sitteth in the temple of God, shewing himself
that he is God.[55]

What could be clearer to indicate that the kingdom of
evil would now invade the very sanctuary of the Church,
and through the very medium of the Church would falsely
project its deceptive program, under the guise of the institution of the Church of God? This usurpation, according
to Paul, would come subsequent to the time which he then
spoke of but before the second coming of Jesus Christ.

This usurpation was later revealed to Joseph Smith:

> . . . for we beheld Satan, . . . who rebelled against
> God, and sought to take the kingdom of our God and his
> Christ—[56]

Of vital importance is the next declaration of Paul to
the saints in that city, for he reminded them,

> And now ye know what withholdeth that he might
> be revealed in his time (or the reason Lucifer had not
> already taken over).
>
> For the mystery of iniquity doth already work: only he
> who now letteth will let, (or will prevent, referring with-
> out question to the apostles of Jesus Christ, with the
> Holy Priesthood, who were still upon the earth), until he
> be taken out of the way (or until they, the apostles,
> were all expired, or out of the way).[57] See also note at
> bottom of page.

Lucifer's Plan to Frustrate God's Work Most Comprehensive

Thus, from the beginning of man's mortal probation
here upon the earth, wicked men have sought, under the
influence of the spirit of rebellion and opposition, fostered
by Satan or Lucifer, as in the pre-existent state, the use of
the dominion of force to suppress men's rights and agency,

---

[55]2 Thess. 2:3-4.
[56]D&C 76:28.
[57]2 Thess. 2:6-8.
Notes: Farrar Could Not Explain. Reference is made to this incident
by Farrar in his Life and Work of St. Paul, pp. 348-351, wherein he proclaimed
that he was content to say with St. Augustine, "I confess that I am entirely
ignorant what the apostle meant."

to gain personal and political ascendancy. Unfortunately, this same power of unrighteous dominion has been exercised by the so-called Christian church in the post-apostolic period, evidencing the craftiness of Satan in leading men astray to their doom through such religious channels which, while purporting to teach truth, misled its followers with practices and doctrines of error.

Wherever this unjust force is imposed by institutions, governments, or churches, it can have but one source of motivation, regardless of how it is colored to appear otherwise,—that of evil, prompted and directed by the kingdom of evil that exists to wield a wicked influence upon the earth.

Priestcrafts in Our Own Day and Time

We need not confine our search for these evidences, to ancient times only, although some reference could be made in passing, to the priestcrafts and secret combinations, which dissoluted a once white and delightsome people, in ancient America, to that of base savagery. From a people highly cultured in the arts of civilization, blessed with a knowledge of God and of the functioning of the priesthood, to that of roaming bands of maddened warriors seeking to kill and caring not whether they were killed. The record of the Book of Mormon is a stark testimony of the abuses of the rights of man, which Lucifer succeeded in establishing among the Nephites and Lamanites and other peoples of Ancient America.

The Influence of Friedrich Nietzsche—Karl Marx

But let us observe our own day and time for further evidences of the diabolical plan of Lucifer and his kingdom of evil to deceive the whole world. Unfortunately for those of us who live today, two men who were contemporary, lived to place into the hands of corrupt leaders basic philosophies of government and the control of the masses, which on careful study bear the unmistakable marks of the doctrines which Lucifer introduced to the children of Adam. These two men, Karl Marx and

Friedrich Nietzsche, (1818-1883, 1844-1900 approx.) while long since dead now, the latter a suicide, their doctrines of evil still continue to exercise unjust powers over the peoples of the earth. From Nietzsche, as his teachings found place in the warped mind of one Adolph Hitler, the world met the effects of Nazism head-on, the result,—50 million deaths, the slaughter to gain ascendance—still the teachings that Cain and Lamech believed in. Still the functioning of the kingdom of evil as it finds means of expression through corrupt government, controlled and dictated by the few who had been taken possession of by the unembodied servants of Lucifer, or who themselves were evil agents unto the master planner, Satan.

From Karl Marx has come the communistic form of government that menaces our present-day world with the doctrines of force and elimination of the gospel of Jesus Christ with faith in a personal God, instilling a hatred for all men that do not subscribe to the doctrines of Marxism. It is a question as to how long it will be until mankind will feel the full impact of this evil-inspired ideology, which opposes all that is righteous and good. The kingdom of evil continues its efforts in this manner to frustrate the plan of God through governments which deal with principles of force to achieve its ends.

Comments by Communist Leaders on Christianity and Religion

Religion is the sigh of the oppressed creature, the sentiment of a heartless world, as it is the spirit of spiritless conditions. It is the opium of the people.[58]

We must combat religion—this is the ABC of all materialism, and consequently Marxism.[59]

We hate Christians and Christianity. Even the best of them must be considered our worst enemies. They preach love of one's neighbor and mercy, which is contrary to our principles. Christian love is an obstacle to the development of the Revolution. Down with love

---

[58]Karl Marx.
[59]Lenin.

of our neighbor! What we want is hate. . . . Only then can we conquer the universe.[60]

We said at the beginning . . . Marxism cannot be conceived without atheism. We would add here that atheism without Marxism is incomplete and inconsistent.[61]

It is impossible to conquer an enemy without having learned to hate him with all the might of one's soul.[62]

There can be no doubt about the fact that the new state of the USSR is led by the Communist Party, with a program permeated by the spirit of militant atheism.[63]

We do not believe in eternal morality, and we expose all the fables about morality.[64]

Every Leninist, every Communist, every class-conscious worker and peasant must be able to explain why a Communist cannot support religion; why Communists fight against religion.[65]

A young man or woman cannot be a Communist unless he or she is free of religious convictions.[66]

The struggle against the Gospel and Christian legend must be conducted ruthlessly and with all the means at the disposal of Communism.[67]

The fight against religion must not be limited nor reduced to abstract ideological preaching. This struggle must be linked up with the concrete, practical class movement; its aim must be to eliminate the social roots of religion.[68]

It is significant to point out that the influence of the philosophy and teachings of two men conceived in evil as their concepts were, should exert their influences and power among men upon the earth, contemporary with the time that the Dispensation of the Fulness of Times inspired and directed of God, should be established upon the earth, (1818-1883, 1844-1900).

------

[60]Anatole Lunarcharsky, Russian Commissar of Education.
[61]Lenin.
[62]Joseph Stalin. Real name: Joseph Vissarionovich Djugashvili.
[63]Yaroslavsky, *Religion in the USSR.*
[64]Lenin.
[65]E. Yaroslavsky, *op. cit.*
[66]Lenin.
[67]Radio Leningrad, August 27, 1950.
[68]Lenin. From *Mercury* (Sept. 1959.)

Lucifer "Deceiveth the Whole World"

Lucifer has, with deception, invaded other channels, for as the Apostle John saw,—"he deceiveth the whole world,"—his plans are carefully worked out in many ways to make it difficult for man to learn truth. Capitalizing on the well-known fact of teaching error, and when not compared with truth, then, the error to those who have blindly accepted it, becomes the truth—Satan has caused erroneous concepts of the philosophy of life itself to be skilfully worked into the religious systems of the world.

A careful study of all religions will reveal the startling fact that the world lacks the fundamental truth, with regard to,

(1) *A knowledge about the true and living God!*

(2) *A knowledge of the true purpose of earth life! and who cannot answer the questions, Whence am I? Who am I? Whither am I going?*

The confusion that exists among men concerning these two important phases of our existence indicates that a very great part of mankind upon the earth and the disembodied spirits, in the spirit world, are misled and simply do not know the truth concerning God and the purpose and destiny of man. This is being cunningly kept from them by the false philosophies and teachings among men. It is difficult to make progress with this maze of error and deception that has descended upon man from the antiquities of a false past.

Here is a chart study of the

PARALLELS OF PERVERSION

As Instituted by Lucifer to Frustrate God's Plan

GOD-INSPIRED TRUTH	LUCIFER-INFLUENCED PERVERSION OF TRUTH
God the Father—God the Son God the Holy Ghost. Persons of Form and Substance, Individual and Distinct Re:—Statement of Joseph Smith the Prophet D&C Section 130	*Trinity of God* compounded into one Personage of same ethereal substance and are incorporeal Re:—Nicene Creed. Statement of Christian churches of World.
Holy Priesthood Power to act in God's name Prophets—Apostles (A) A true right to represent God. (B) Ordinances administered are made efficacious. (C) Glorification or Exaltation through keys of power bestowed in proper manner. (D) Continuity of this power through rightful succession and righteousness. Re:—D&C 121:41-43 PofGP, Moses 5:9 D&C 112	*Priestcraft* Usurped right to represent God—False ministers (A) Ordinances and rituals without authority not binding, mockery to God. (B) No exaltation—keys and laws non-operative (C) Continuity of priestcraft through error and deception. (D) Use of unrighteous dominion. Re:—D&C 121:36-37 PofGP, Moses 5:29-52 D&C 1:35
Holy Sacrament Emblems of Remembrance. Renewal of Covenant. Re:—D&C 20 Last Supper.	*Holy Sacrament* Emblems of Transmutation. Attended by Ritual. Re:—See other Christian churches
Salvation for the Dead (A) Christ the mediator. (B) Vicarious service here. (C) Gospel preached in spirit world— Voluntary acceptance. (D) Exercise of given rights to seal and bind—Predicated on gospel law of gifts. Re:—D&C Sections 124, 127, 128 D&C Section 132 (Advocate) D&C Sections 29, 110, 76, 107	*Prayers for the Dead* (A) The Virgin Mary. (B) Patron Saints to intercede. (C) Purgatory and monetary penance. (D) Other methods of tribute to pagan god and idols appeasements to satisfy. Re:—Catholic doctrines pagan customs

PARALLELS OF PERVERSION

TRUTH	PERVERSION OF TRUTH

Repentance

(A) Confession.
(B) Forsaking forever.
(C) Release of emotional stress.
(D) Laws of God and Church.
(E) Repeated violation brings severance.

Re:—D&C 58.

Confession and Penance

(A) Frequent confession of same sin.
(B) Repeated violation of God's laws.
(C) Indulgences.
(D) Monetary connection with forgiveness.
(E) Repentance as a gesture both pagan and Catholic.
(F) Festive periods followed by penance.

Atonement of Christ

(A) Vicarious sacrifice
(B) Immortal Sire ⎫ Power
(C) Virgin Mother ⎭
(D) Gift of Eternal Life for the resurrected body. (Universal.)
(E) The reconciliation of the soul. (The gospel.)
(F) Obedience and conformity to God's will.

Re:—D&C 76:20-24
      D&C—76:69
      BofM—Alma 21
      PofGP—Moses 5:9; 4:2
      D&C 109:4
      BofM—Mosiah 4:2-6

Other Crucified Saviors

1.	Chrishna—India	1200 BC.
2.	Sakia—Hindoo	600 BC.
3.	Thammuz—Syria	1160 BC.
4.	Wittoba—Teungonese	552 BC.
5.	Iao—Nepal	622 BC.
6.	Hesus—Celtic	834 BC.
7.	Thulis—Egypt	1700 BC.
8.	Indra—Tibet	725 BC.
9.	Gautama—Bhuddist	480 BC.
10.	Crite—Chaldea	1200 BC.
11.	Atys—Phrygia	1170 BC.
12.	Mithra—Persia	600 B.C.

Re:—Claims of miraculous
Many   or virgin births—
others   Gautama—Ray of
every   starlight—all
nation   crucified in one way
and   or another for sins of
people.   fellow men.

Sacrifice for Sin

(A) Voluntary death to fulfil atonement.
(B) To initiate the way.

Human Sacrifice

(A) To appease false gods.
(B) Egypt—Chaldea—Abraham.
(C) Lamanites.
(D) Mystic rites—Sacrifice of virgins.

Salvation and Exaltation

(A) Gospel plan—Resurrection.
(B) Degrees of glory.
(C) Many mansions.
(D) Man to be governed by that law he can abide.
(E) The eternity of the soul.
(F) Constant endeavor and growth.
(G) Godhood.

Heaven and State of Rest

(A) The body is evil.
(B) Two states only.
(C) The Karma—Cosmic Spirit.
(D) Forced into submission, part of all-pervading spirit.
(E) The loss of the body.
(F) Re-incarnation to state of endless sameness.

PARALLELS OF PERVERSION

TRUTH	PERVERSION OF TRUTH
Also Resurrection Body and Spirit—Soul.	*Re-incarnation* Body evil, to be discarded.

COMMENT

Thus it can be seen in the establishing of the false counterparts—the perversions, in every crucial phase of God's plan, Lucifer builds up a vast deception, which, as the years extend into centuries, antiquities with time each custom and practice—and as it burns its way into the minds of men, they are deceived. Man himself, lost in the maze of perverted truth, cannot learn the truth. It requires revelation from God—the source of truth—through an appointed prophet to make it known. Such a key of knowledge, or truth, is always given to the priesthood of God, which priesthood is also bestowed under the direction of Christ, for it is after his order. The priesthood, when functioning upon the earth, possesses the key of knowledge, thereby providing man with the channels of truth, which, if adhered to, will break down the perversions of truth with which Lucifer seeks to deceive and confuse the children of God.

Righteous Dominion as Compared with Unrighteous Dominion

The Prophet Joseph Smith, while confined in Liberty Jail received a communication from God which tells of the differences between the principles of righteous dominion and that of unrighteous dominion. These are given here.

That the rights of the priesthood are inseparably connected with the powers of heaven, and that the powers of heaven cannot be controlled nor handled only upon the principles of righteousness.

Unrighteous Dominion

That they may be conferred upon us, it is true; but when we undertake to (a) *cover our sins,* or to (b) *gratify our pride,* our (c) *vain ambition,* or to exercise control or (d) *dominion or compulsion* upon the souls of the children of men, in (e) *any degree of unrighteousness,* behold, the heavens withdraw themselves; the Spirit of the Lord is grieved; and when it is withdrawn, Amen to the priesthood or the authority of that man.[69]

------

[69]D&C 121:36-37.

Summarized

1. To cover our sins.
2. Gratify pride.
3. Vain ambition.
4. Compulsion.
5. Unrighteousness (many degrees).

Righteous Dominion

No power or influence can or ought to be maintained by virtue of the priesthood, only by (a) *persuasion,* by (b) *long-suffering,* by (c) *gentleness and meekness,* and by (d) *love unfeigned;*

By (e) *kindness,* and (f) *pure knowledge,* which shall greatly enlarge the soul without hypocrisy, and without guile—

(g) *Reproving betimes with sharpness,* when moved upon by the Holy Ghost; and then showing forth afterwards an increase of *love* toward him whom thou hast reproved, lest he esteem thee to be his enemy; . . .[70]

Summarized

1. Persuasion.
2. Long-suffering.
3. Gentleness and meekness.
4. Love *Unfeigned.*
5. Kindness.
6. Pure knowledge.
7. Reproving with *love.*

Comment

Unrighteous dominion in any form, whether exercised by governmental administration, through religious or other social groups, or through institutions of any kind, including labor unions or lodges, which provide a channel of dealing with people, any suppression of human right, or tendency, any application of unjust force upon the individual, without permitting him the right of choice, whereby he may exercise his agency, which is God-given, is a tool

---

[70]*Ibid.,* 121:41-43.

of evil, influenced and motivated by the powers of the kingdom of evil, of which Lucifer is the leader, that has invaded our dominion of human life.

The Glory of the Doctrine of Agency

The agency of man is not a power to be left dormant or itself to be moved upon solely by exterior forces for good or evil. Man in the true sense of the meaning is "agent unto himself," and, therefore, should assume the prerogative of acting as a result of his own volition for and in behalf of himself. This great principle is explained most effectively in one of the revelations given to the Prophet Joseph Smith. At one time, in the early days of the Church, some of the members thought that because the Prophet was in frequent contact with the Lord in the necessary bringing forth of many principles and laws in establishing and governing the Church, that their every individual action was to be directed by revelation, both as to the Church, and for each member. While some of the early revelations were given to individuals, the Lord soon let it be known, that when a principle was revealed, or a condition explained or a law invoked, that the members of the Church should subscribe to it of their own free will in the exercise of their agency.

Not only this, but that they should themselves pursue a volitional course of righteousness, by interpreting what they had already received, in the way of truth, and choosing within themselves to go forward and do good. In this, as the Lord explained, is contained the real efficacy of *agency*. Let us examine the words of the Lord on this very principle,

> For behold, it is not meet that I should command in all things; for he that is compelled in all things, the same is a slothful and not a wise servant; wherefore he receiveth no reward.
>
> Verily I say, men should be anxiously engaged in a good cause, and do many things of their own free will, and bring to pass much righteousness;
>
> For the power is in them, wherein they are agents

unto themselves. And inasmuch as men do good they
shall in nowise lose their reward.

But he that doeth not anything until he is commanded, and receiveth a commandment with doubtful
heart, and keepeth it with slothfulness, the same is
damned.[71]

Man Reaches Apex of Greatness in Choosing
Good over Evil

For man to know good and evil, such as the Gods do,[72]
and then by virtue of choice or agency, choose the good
rather than the evil, becomes the crowning achievement
of the individual in this mortal existence. As each individual learns and applies this law in his life, the mission
and calling of Jesus Christ is vindicated. In this, when
pursued in accordance with the plan of the gospel, man
shall return to the presence of God, having fulfilled successfully, the purpose of an earth life probation.[73]

In Choosing Evil, Man Is Leagued with
Lucifer as an Evil Agent

In the exercise of agency, where man chooses to follow
evil rather than good, such as it was, in varying degrees
with those who followed Lucifer in the pre-existence and
also as with the sons of Adam who disobeyed God and
hearkened unto the teachings of Lucifer, he himself can
become an agency of evil, to promote this influence within
the perimeter of his existence, be he a servant, a king, or
dictator. Cain, the son of Adam, developed evil tendencies,
whereas as a master of lies and deceit, and because of his
rejection of God, he became a son of perdition. Yet, he
will have a resurrected body, and because of such will be
above Lucifer. But had Cain repented, he would have
escaped this punishment; for unto Cain the Lord said,

If thou doest well, thou shalt be accepted. And if
thou doest not well, sin lieth at the door, and Satan
desireth to have thee; and except thou shalt hearken unto
my commandments, I will deliver thee up, and it shall be

---

[71]*Ibid.*, 58:26-29.
[72]Gen. 3:22.
[73]P. of G. P., Abraham 3:25-26.

unto thee according to his desire. *And thou shalt rule over him;*

For from this time forth thou shalt be the father of his lies; thou shalt be called Perdition; for thou wast also before the world.[74]

In explaining further how man himself can become an agent of evil, and in speaking of the going forth of false spirits upon the earth, the Lord made known the following to the Prophet Joseph Smith:

. . . that ye may not be seduced by evil spirits, or doctrines of devils, *or the commandments of men; for some are of men,* and others of devils.[75]

Evil Disembodied Spirits Continue Their Evil in Their Own Spheres

Such evil men or women when they die and are sent to the state of disembodiment waiting the day of judgment and resurrection, continue their evil practices and tendencies in that place of their confinement in the spirit world. Concerning these, Brigham Young has said,

There are myriads of disembodied evil spirits—those who have long ago laid down their bodies—here and in regions round about, among and around us; and they are trying to make us and our children sick, and are trying to destroy us and tempt us to evil. They will try every possible means they are masters of to draw us aside from the path of righteousness.[76]

These personages, who have become evil agents unto themselves in this life, join the evil band of Lucifer and his kingdom of evil, to oppose God and his plan of righteousness. They, of course, in the final judgment, will continue to be with him as sons and daughters of perdition. Their place of habitation, after all is done with, concerning the probation of life, is given in a revelation to the Prophet Joseph Smith. After having designated the

---

[74]P. of G.P., Moses 5:23-24.
[75]D&C 46:7.
[76]*Discourses of Brigham Young,* p. 110.

three kingdoms of glory, (a) celestial (b) terrestrial (c) telestial, as the places where each one can abide such a kingdom of glory, the Lord reveals the place where others, not of these three kingdoms, or glories, will reside.

> For he who is not able to abide the law of a celestial kingdom cannot abide a celestial glory.
> And he who cannot abide the law of a terrestrial kingdom cannot abide a terrestrial glory.
> And he who cannot abide the law of a telestial kingdom cannot abide a telestial glory; therefore he is not meet for a kingdom of glory. *Therefore he must abide a kingdom which is not a kingdom of glory.*[77]

The Awful Fate of Those of Perdition Not Known

With further reference to the sons and daughters of perdition, who have been embodied in this probation, but who, after having received of the testimony of Jesus by direct manifestation from the Holy Ghost, deny it and openly oppose the will and work of God, these shall dwell in their own kingdom, the exact conditions concerning which we are not given to know, but the Lord has said the following:

> Thus saith the Lord concerning all those who know my power, and have been made partakers thereof, and suffered themselves through the power of the devil to be overcome, *and to deny the truth, and defy my power—*
> They are they who are the sons of perdition, of whom I say that it had been better for them never to have been born; (or the purpose of the probation of mortality will not be fulfilled in them.)
> For they are vessels of wrath, doomed to suffer the wrath of God, with the devil and his angels in eternity; . . .
> And the only ones on whom the second death shall have any power;
> Yea, verily, the only ones who shall not be redeemed in the due time of the Lord, after the sufferings of his wrath.
> For all the rest shall be brought forth by the resurrection of the dead, *through the triumph and the glory of*

---

[77]D&C 88:22-24.

the Lamb, who was slain, who was in the bosom of the Father, before the worlds were made. . . . (i.e.—All the rest shall find the true benefits of the resurrection, in being placed in one or another of the three glories, as a result of the atoning sacrifice of Christ, but these, the sons of perdition, shall suffer the *second death,* which means they will forever be shut out of the presence of God, in the celestial, Jesus Christ in the terrestrial, or the priesthood in the telestial, speaking from an administrative basis).

Wherefore, he saves all except them—they shall go away into everlasting punishment which is endless punishment, which is eternal punishment, to reign with the devil and his angels in eternity, . . .

And the end thereof, neither the place thereof, nor their torment, no man knows;

Neither was it revealed, neither is, neither will be revealed unto man except to them who are made partakers thereof;[78]

A Frightening Realization

The frightening realization of this condition with the power of evil in the world, brings this question, What are we to do? Is there a definite way of escape from the deceptions of the kingdom of evil? Obviously there is; there was in the beginning, in the pre-existent world, for let us remember, that while many followed after Lucifer, being deceived by him, through their own inclinations of wickedness, there were still two-thirds of the hosts of heaven that did not follow him. These have and will be tabernacled in the flesh in this probation, and have the privilege and opportunity given them, each one, to rise above this evil force, to work out their own salvation.

A Plan of Redemption Prepared

Before the foundation of the earth was laid, before man was placed upon it, the plan of salvation was studied and known by all. It was in rebellion to this plan that Lucifer sought to aggrandize himself and was cast out of the presence of God; while in obedience to it, the Only Begotten sought to do the will of the Father. The will

---

[78]*Ibid.,* 76:31-33, 37-39, 44-46.

of the Father provided that man could go through the
experience of the "fall" or a spiritual separation from God
the Father, known as death, and could yet return back to
the presence of God, and future realms of growth and
expansion.

Unto Adam and Eve, in the early days of their experience upon the earth, subsequent to the events that led
to their mortality, there began to be born sons and daughters, and these sons and daughters divided two by two and
themselves had other children. The births and expansion
of this first family were contemporary with the enticings
of Lucifer and his establishment of priestcraft. An angel
of the Lord asked Adam and Eve why they offered sacri-
fices unto the Lord; their answer was simple, since the
Lord had instructed them to do so at the time of the expulsion from the Garden of Eden.

> And Adam said unto him: I know not, save the Lord
> commanded me.[79]

The angel then advised them that this was done as a
similitude of the sacrifice of the Only Begotten of the
Father, and that whatever they would do should be done
in the name of the Son. Upon this occasion the principle
of repentance was introduced. (Actually this was the
beginning of the priesthood, which God bestowed upon
Adam anew, which power is a restraining force against
evil.)

In that day the Holy Ghost fell upon Adam, and bore
record of the Father and the Son, saying:

> . . . I am the Only Begotten of the Father from the be-
> ginning, henceforth and forever, that as thou hast fallen
> thou mayest be redeemed, *and all mankind, even
> as many as will.*[80]

With this knowledge conveyed unto them, Adam
blessed the name of God and prophesied concerning all the

---

[79]P. of G. P., Moses 5:6.
[80]*Ibid.*, 5:9.

families of the earth.   Both he and Eve rejoiced, for said they,

> . . . Were it not for our transgression we never should have had seed, and never should have known good and evil, and the joy of our redemption, and the eternal life which God giveth unto all the obedient."[81]

The Saving Principle of Repentance

In speaking of this life and the space granted for man to repent, that they might return unto God, Alma, a Book of Mormon prophet, has this to say, which also is in confirmation of the teachings of Amulek,

> And we see that death comes upon mankind, yea, the death which has been spoken of by Amulek, which is the temporal death; nevertheless there was a space granted unto man in which he might *repent;* therefore this life became a probationary state; a time to prepare to meet God; a time to prepare for that endless state which has been spoken of by us, which is after the resurrection. . . .[82]

God's Plan to Have His Children Back with Him

The protective plan of salvation is twofold. It involves first, universal salvation, which comes to all mankind regardless of race, color, or creed. The mere fact that men have been born into this life qualifies them for the application of this universal gift, which is made possible by the atoning sacrifice of Jesus Christ.

The atonement of Christ made possible by initiation and power, that man could experience the fall and yet live again as a resurrected personage. Thus the imposition of death cast upon all mankind by the fall of our first parents, is atoned for and this unconditionally. It is a gift of God through his Only Begotten Son. This is what is termed *universal salvation.*

Individual salvation concerns the personal worthiness of the individual as he learns through sacrifice and obedi-

---

[81]*Ibid.*, 5:11.
[82]Alma 12:24.

ence by his own volition to choose righteousness rather than sin and error. It is in this personal struggle that Lucifer attempts to deceive and dissuade. He can do nothing about the other. But, in personal salvation, as also in universal salvation, there is a way that has been provided by God our Heavenly Father. Our Elder Brother, Jesus Christ, is the author of this plan.[83]

And through him only, comes personal salvation.[84]

The gospel plan of personal salvation is found in obedience to certain laws and commandments which have been given by the author of the plan, Jesus Christ, as stated, and as this plan is applied. There is a spiritual power connected with the gospel which is the witness unto all who receive it. This power will ever provide a personal protection in our search for the true endowment of life. This power actually must be more than a physical knowledge, it is a communion of the spirit with our Heavenly Father, with the Holy Ghost testifying unto us by confirmation of obedience by choice to the commandments of God.

The Power of Change
Rebirth unto Righteousness

This inward force, and of its need for spiritual rebirth, is taught most convincingly to Nicodemus by the Savior, when upon an occasion this much disturbed Jewish leader, a member of the Sanhedrin, came to the Christ in search of wisdom. The Christ taught him what the motivating power of conviction really was. But it was too difficult for the learned lawyer to understand, for it involved the subtle implications of the Spirit. The Christ said unto him in answer to his question concerning eternal life.

> Marvel not that I said unto thee, Ye must be born again.
> The wind bloweth where it listeth, and thou hearest the sound thereof, but canst not tell whence it cometh, and

---

[83]P. of G. P., Moses 5:9; 4:2.
[84]D&C 109:4; Mosiah 4:2-6.

whither it goeth: *So is everyone that is born of the Spirit.*[85]

Nicodemus was even more confused at this statement, for he was thinking of some sort of physical rebirth, and the Christ was speaking of an inward change. Christ then chided him with,

Art thou a master of Israel, and knowest not these things?[86]

The Power and Necessity of Testimony

And thus it is, the power of conviction, the power of inward change, a change for the better made possible through repentance. And in repentance we see exhibited the very highest form of agency, for a man to repent truly, must within himself will it so; it must be voluntary or it is no repentance at all; and when it is voluntary, it represents the individual selection of right over wrong. This would not be possible if man did not or could not know the difference. Thus we see the whole plan of life and salvation as it affects the individual, based on the fundamental requirement of agency.

The Apostle John on the Isle of Patmos saw this also, for he saw the overcoming of Lucifer and his kingdom, first by the atoning sacrifice of Jesus Christ as to *universal salvation,* and the *testimony of the saints* as to *personal salvation.* Ponder this statement of John,

And they overcame him, (meaning Lucifer who had been cast down upon the earth,) *by the blood of the Lamb, and by the word of their testimony;*[87]

What is testimony? It is the rock of the Church. It is the *power* that binds man and God together, while he sojourns here in this life. It requires the administration of the Holy Ghost to obtain it and requires conformity to

[85]John 3:7-8.
[86]*Ibid.,* 3:10.
[87]Rev. 12:11.

gospel principles to keep it. Every time a man bears his testimony of the divinity of Jesus Christ, of Joseph Smith, a true prophet of God, and of the true Church of Jesus Christ upon the earth, there is a miracle taking place. Man need have no fear of evil, if his testimony is alive—if he is not borrowing from a bygone inspiration. If the Holy Ghost is bearing witness to him today, this very minute, then, he is in tune with God. *This then is how evil is to be overcome.*

Section Three

The Day of the Gentile

COMMENTS REGARDING CHART

Professed Christianity in the world today, while twice as large as the next religious concept, represents only about 31% of the world's population. In Asia, a great gentile area, only 3% of the population profess to be Christians. Of these covenant descendants of Japheth, 329 million are Hindus, 300 million Confucians, and about 150 million Buddhists, with 50 million Taoists and 50 million Shintoists.

Of the covenant house of Judah, there are 12 million Jews, with 5 million of these in America. Add to this the 481 million, a group twice as large as North America combined who follow some minor cult or no religion at all as also the 121 million followers of primitive and tribal religions, mainly in Africa.

The world's Christian religions total about 870 million; of these 528 million are reported to be Catholic, 213 million Protestant, of which there are 254 denominations, and 129 million Eastern Orthodox or Greek Catholic.

Submerged in these many millions, is the Church and kingdom of God, the Church of Jesus Christ of Latter-day Saints, with about 2 million members, but which adheres to the declaration of the Master who once proclaimed:

> Strait is the gate, and narrow is the way, which leadeth unto life, and *few* there be that find it. (Matt. 7:14.)

Neither Catholic, Protestant, or Jew, but the Church of Jesus Christ restored in these latter days, unto whom has come the divine commitment from the Lord to declare unto the world, that millions more may yet accept, the truths of the everlasting gospel of Jesus Christ, now revealed again, for the purpose declared in a revelation from God,

> They seek not the Lord to establish his righteousness, but every man walketh in his own way, and after the image of his own God, whose image is in the likeness of the

world, and whose substance is that of an idol, which waxeth old and shall perish in Babylon, even Babylon the great, which shall fall.

Wherefore, I the Lord, knowing the calamity which should come upon the inhabitants of the earth, called upon my servant Joseph Smith, Jun., and spake unto him from heaven, and gave him commandments;

And also gave commandments to others, that they should proclaim these things unto the world; and all this that it might be fulfilled, which was written by the prophets—

The weak things of the world shall come forth and break down the mighty and strong ones, that man should not counsel his fellow man, neither trust in the arm of flesh—

But that every man might speak in the name of God the Lord, even the Savior of the world;

That faith also might increase in the earth;

That mine everlasting covenant might be established;

That the fulness of my gospel might be proclaimed by the weak and the simple unto the ends of the world, and before kings and rulers. (D&C 1:16-23.)

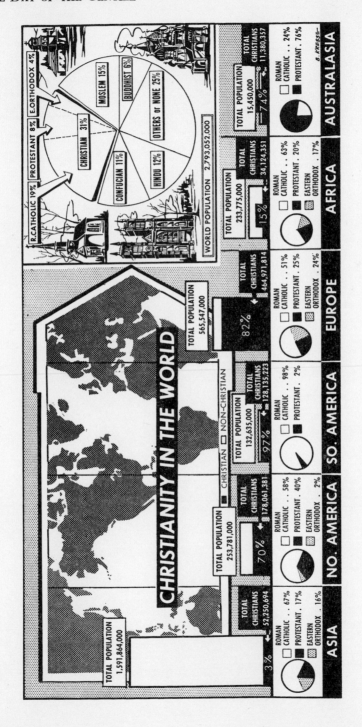

CHRISTIANITY IN THE WORLD

WORLD POPULATION 2,793,052,000

MOSLEM 15%
BUDDHIST 6%
OTHERS or NONE 25%
HINDU 12%
CONFUCIAN 11%
CHRISTIAN 31%
E. ORTHODOX 4%
PROTESTANT 8%
R. CATHOLIC 19%

CHRISTIAN ☐ NON-CHRISTIAN

AUSTRALASIA
TOTAL POPULATION 15,450,000
TOTAL CHRISTIANS 11,380,357
74%
ROMAN CATHOLIC .. 24%
PROTESTANT . 76%

AFRICA
TOTAL POPULATION 233,775,000
TOTAL CHRISTIANS 34,124,351
15%
ROMAN CATHOLIC .. 63%
PROTESTANT . 20%
EASTERN ORTHODOX . 17%

EUROPE
TOTAL POPULATION 565,547,000
TOTAL CHRISTIANS 464,971,814
82%
ROMAN CATHOLIC .. 51%
PROTESTANT . 25%
EASTERN ORTHODOX . 24%

SO. AMERICA
TOTAL POPULATION 132,635,000
TOTAL CHRISTIANS 128,135,223
97%
ROMAN CATHOLIC .. 98%
PROTESTANT . 2%

NO. AMERICA
TOTAL POPULATION 253,781,000
TOTAL CHRISTIANS 178,061,381
70%
ROMAN CATHOLIC .. 58%
PROTESTANT . 40%
EASTERN ORTHODOX . 2%

ASIA
TOTAL POPULATION 1,591,864,000
TOTAL CHRISTIANS 52,250,694
3%
ROMAN CATHOLIC .. 67%
PROTESTANT . 17%
EASTERN ORTHODOX . 16%

G. KRESSE

The Day of the Gentile

When Moses left the children of Israel encamped at the base of Mount Sinai and ascended the mountain, he was met by Lucifer who tried to deceive and prevent him from receiving further communication from God, the Father, and his Son, Jesus Christ. In fact, Lucifer proclaimed himself, upon that occasion, to be the son of God and demanded that Moses fall down and worship him, because in addition to being the "only begotten" he was also the God of this world, and that if Moses would do this, he would receive great personal honor and glory. Lucifer promised all these things to deceive him. But Moses sensed and detected that he was being deceived and told Lucifer how he had perceived the deception and that he knew who he was.

> And it came to pass that when Moses had said these words, behold, Satan came tempting him, saying: Moses, son of man, worship me.
>
> And it came to pass that Moses looked upon Satan and said: Who art thou? For behold, I am a son of God, in the similitude of his Only Begotten; and where is thy glory, that I should worship thee?
>
> For behold, I could not look upon God, except his glory should come upon me, and I were strengthened before him. But I can look upon thee in the natural man. Is it not so, surely?
>
> Blessed be the name of my God, for his Spirit hath not altogether withdrawn from me, or else where is thy glory, for it is darkness unto me? And I can judge between thee and God; for God said unto me: Worship God, for him only shalt thou serve.
>
> Get thee hence, Satan; deceive me not; for God said unto me: Thou art after the similitude of mine Only Begotten.
>
> And he also gave me commandments when he called unto me out of the burning bush, saying: Call upon God in the name of mine Only Begotten, and worship me.
>
> And again Moses said: I will not cease to call upon God, I have other things to inquire of him: for his glory

has been upon me, wherefore I can judge between him
and thee. Depart hence, Satan.

And now, when Moses had said these words, Satan
cried with a loud voice, and rent upon the earth, and
commanded, saying: I am the Only Begotten, worship me.

And it came to pass that Moses began to fear exceedingly; and as he began to fear, he saw the bitterness
of hell. Nevertheless, calling upon God, he received
strength, and he commanded, saying: Depart from me,
Satan, for this one God only will I worship, which is the
God of glory.

And now Satan began to tremble, and the earth shook;
and Moses received strength, and called upon God, saying: in the name of the Only Begotten, depart hence,
Satan.

And it came to pass that Satan cried with a loud
voice, with weeping, and wailing, and gnashing of teeth;
and he departed hence, even from the presence of Moses,
that he beheld him not.

And now of this thing Moses bore record; but because
of wickedness it is not had among the children of men.

And it came to pass that when Satan had departed
from the presence of Moses, that Moses lifted up his eyes
unto heaven, being filled with the Holy Ghost, which
beareth record of the Father and the Son.[1]

It was then that Lucifer tried to overpower and
destroy him. Had it not been for Michael or Adam, our
first father in the flesh, who had been associated with God
the Father and his Son, in the creation of the earth, coming
to the rescue of Moses, he might have forfeited his life.
This experience is similar to that which the Prophet Joseph
Smith had in the Sacred Grove when he related his own
experience with the powers of darkness.

> . . . I was seized upon by some power which entirely
> overcame me, and had such an astonishing influence
> over me as to bind my tongue so that I could not speak.
> Thick darkness gathered around me, and it seemed to me
> for a time as if I were doomed to sudden destruction.
>
> But, exerting all my powers to call upon God to
> deliver me out of the power of this enemy which had
> seized upon me, and at the very moment when I was

---

[1]P. of G. P., Moses 1:12-24.

ready to sink into despair and abandon myself to destruction—not to an imaginary ruin, but to the power of some actual being from the unseen world, who had such marvelous power as I had never before felt in any being—just at this moment of great alarm, I saw a pillar of light exactly over my head, above the brightness of the sun, which descended gradually until it fell upon me.

It no sooner appeared than I found myself delivered from the enemy which held me bound. When the light rested upon me I saw two Personages, whose brightness and glory defy all description, standing above me in the air. One of them spake unto me, calling me by name and said, pointing to the other—This is My Beloved Son. Hear Him![2]

The Evil Power of Lucifer Manifest in Other Dispensations

Not only was the evil influence and person of Lucifer felt in the Sacred Grove, but his presence and person had also been felt in attempting to prevent the opening of other dispensations. In the dispensation of Adam,

And Satan came among them, saying: I am also a son of God; and he commanded them, saying: Believe it not; and they believed it not, and they loved Satan more than God. And men began from that time forth to be carnal, sensual, and devilish.[3]

In the Dispensation of Enoch,

And he beheld Satan; and he had a great chain in his hand, and it veiled the whole face of the earth with darkness; and he looked up and laughed, and his angels rejoiced.[4]

In the Dispensation of the Meridian of Time,

Then was Jesus led up of the spirit into the wilderness to be tempted of the devil.

And when he had fasted forty days and forty nights, he was afterward an hungred.

And when the tempter came to him, he said, If thou be the Son of God, command that these stones be made bread.

---

[2]P. of G.P., Joseph Smith 2:15-17.
[3]P. of G. P., Moses 5:13.
[4]*Ibid.*, 7:26.

But he answered and said, It is written, Man shall
not live by bread alone, but by every word that pro-
ceedeth out of the mouth of God.

Then the devil taketh him up into the holy city, and
setteth him on a pinnacle of the temple,

And saith unto him, If thou be the Son of God, cast
thyself down: for it is written, He shall give his angels
charge concerning thee: and in their hands they shall
bear thee up, lest at any time thou dash thy foot against
a stone.

Jesus said unto him, It is written again, Thou shalt not
tempt the Lord thy God.

Again, the devil taketh him up into an exceeding high
mountain, and sheweth him all the kingdoms of the
world, and the glory of them;

And saith unto him, All these things will I give thee,
if thou wilt fall down and worship me.

Then saith Jesus unto him, Get thee hence, Satan:
for it is written, Thou shalt worship the Lord thy God, and
him only shalt thou serve.

Then the devil leaveth him, and, behold, angels came
and ministered unto him.[5]

Lucifer knows full well what the revealing of the
gospel plan means to God's children, and he exerts his
greatest influence whenever a dispensation is given and
tries to prevent it.

The Calling of Michael to Hold Lucifer in Check

But as Lucifer contended with Moses, Adam or
Michael made his appearance and dispelled Lucifer. According to the scriptures we are told that Michael
contended with Lucifer for the body of Moses.

Yet Michael the archangel, when contending with the
devil he disputed about the body of Moses, durst not
bring against him a railing accusation, but said, The Lord
rebuke thee.[6]

And thus by the power of the priesthood he dispelled
Lucifer, thus permitting Moses to be divinely interceded

[5]Matthew 4:1-11.
[6]Jude 9.

with, as given in the scriptural account of God speaking
to Moses out of the burning bush. The bush that was never
consumed apparently happened to be within the area
of the *Light* which appeared with such power that it made
the bush or shrubs appear as if they were on fire. Moses
explained it as a burning bush. But apparently it was a
condition of light which surrounds God the Father and his
Son in their movements. Moses then heard the voice of
God speaking out of the burning bush or actually out of
the light that surrounded and encompassed the bush. It
was not burning in the sense of physical fire. It was a light
in which Holy Personages must be encompassed to appear
here upon the earth. We have an indication of this manifestation of light in the appearance of God the Father and
his Son Jesus Christ to the Prophet Joseph Smith who relates, that suddenly a pillar of light appeared until it rested
upon him, which light was brighter than noonday sun.

The very appearance of this light dispelled the power
of evil that threatened his life. In the light he saw two
Personages, who were God the Father and his Son. Thus
it would seem that whenever divine and holy beings appear to others in mortality they do so in the envelopment
of this light which apparently is a complete protection
against anything that is earthly or carnal.

There are other evidences of this. When Moroni appeared to the Prophet Joseph Smith, a light was discovered
appearing in his room. He describes further that while the
room became exceedingly bright, that it was even brighter
around the immediate person of the heavenly visitor. What
it is that permits these personages from the presence of
God or God himself to come and go and to move at tremendous speeds through space in the element of this light
is one of the mysteries of Godliness.

Further Evidences of This Light

It is to be noted in the Bible further, that when the two
Marys returned to the tomb to complete the anointing
and to finish the wrappings on the body of Jesus, they told

of seeing two men who were guarding the tomb. Here
again we find the recording of this same thing; the appearance of light. They described it as two men in "shining
garments," whereas it was two men sent to guard the tomb
and who stood in this envelopment of light which made
it look as if they wore shining apparel. There are many
other recorded instances where this same thing took place.
(The three Hebrews in the fiery furnace, Daniel 3:23-27,
where this fire of the Spirit or a substance of light was a
protection against physical fire. Consider also the experience of Nephi, 4 Nephi 32; the appearance of angels and
the cloven tongues of fire with the children, as described
in the Book of Mormon, 3 Nephi 17:24; other indications
of the protection of fire are found in Helaman 5:23-25.)

When Moses stood in the presence of God the Father
and his Son, for not only was God the Father present on
Mount Sinai, but also his son, Jesus Christ,[7] he was told
among other things, that the worlds without number had
been created to bring to pass his holy purposes in the redemption of man, and that they were created through the
Son. At that time he was given tablets of stone upon which
was written the gospel of Jesus Christ, to be given to the
Israelites. Moses came down out of the mountain, having
been in the presence of God for an extended period of
time, and having undergone some change in the appearance of his person that permitted this, causing his personage to shine. He stood before them, and as he did so, they
couldn't even look upon him because of the radiance of
his body. This in some way was caused by the same light
that he had partaken of.

He held in his arms the tablets of stone, ready to reveal
to the Israelites the sacred and redeeming first principles
of the gospel. But in the meantime, the children of Israel

---

[7]NOTE: The Old Testament not fully translated states that God only was
there, but latter-day revelation gives us the fuller account and meaning of
what actually took place on the Mount. In this respect it is apparent from the
revelations that what occurred there is similar to that which was experienced
by Joseph Smith in the Sacred Grove, wherein God the Father appeared
and announced his Son who stood by him, by stating, "This is my beloved
Son."

The traditional Mount Sinai where Moses received the Ten Commandments.

had forgotten the God of Israel, and had gone over to pagan worship, openly committing acts of adultery, drunkenness, and all manner of licentiousness. Spurred on by false and weak leaders, who had lost the faith, they put to shame the counsel of Moses, and renounced their noble heritage of their chosen lineage. The extent of their sins against God brought upon them a judgment of destruction. By destruction, it was meant that they were to be destroyed in not being permitted to go into the promised land. Many were stricken with death immediately, while the others, in consequence of this judgment, were driven into the wilderness there to roam until their bodies were wasted away, and until a new generation had been raised up.

Concerning this tragic event in the history of ancient Israel, we are enlightened by the writings of Moses.

A New Generation

After the children of Israel had wandered for thirty-eight years and six months in the desert, every single one of them had died except two, Joshua and Caleb. Joshua was a descendant of Ephraim, Caleb a descendant of Judah; Moses continued with them during this time of exile but did not himself enter the promised land. Thus, at this period there were only three who survived the great number of people who had come out of Egypt. The Lord had now raised up a new generation to enter into the promised land.

After their many wanderings and as the wasting process continued, they had come to the gateway of the promised land, known as Kadesh-Barnea. This is the southernmost gateway into this choice land and may still be identified in that land today. This much-desired area, the most fertile and productive in all that land, had been given unto Abraham and his posterity by covenant. Abraham came upon it as he traveled out of the north by commandment from the Lord from the city of Haran. (The location of this ancient place, and still bearing the same name, is found today in southern Turkey.) He was en

route to Egypt, when he received the commandment to go
there by the Lord, and as he passed through this land, the
Lord gave it to him by covenant. And now the children
of Israel, his posterity, were prepared after all these many
hundreds of years to go into and possess it.

> And I will bring you in unto the land, concerning the
> which I did swear to give it to Abraham, to Isaac, and to
> Jacob; and I will give it you for an heritage: I am the
> Lord.[8]

The Lord had commanded Moses to gather the children of Israel, who were the sons and daughters of those
who had come out of Egypt, in one vast multitude at this
gateway to Caanan, for as such it was known. They had
previously sent spies from each of the twelve tribes into
the land to see how they could best take it, for the occu-
pants of the land would not yield without conflict. They
came back with reports, most of which were negative:
their pronouncements were to the effect that the land could
not possibly be taken. One reason given was that the giants
of Anak occupied it and that these were men of great
stature and were great warriors who would destroy them.
They complained that the Lord had preserved the children
only now to bring them there to be destroyed. But Joshua
and Caleb, the descendants of Ephraim and Judah, favored
the taking of the land. They had the faith that the Lord
God would preserve them, proclaiming that it belonged
to them by covenant. It was at this time that Joshua
courageously declared,

> And Joshua the son of Nun, and Caleb the son of
> Jephunneh, which were of them that searched the land,
> rent their clothes:
> And they spake unto all the company of the children
> of Israel, saying, The land, which we passed through
> to search it, is an exceeding good land.
> If the Lord delight in us, then he will bring us into
> this land, and give it us; a land which floweth with milk
> and honey.

---

[8]Exodus 6:8.

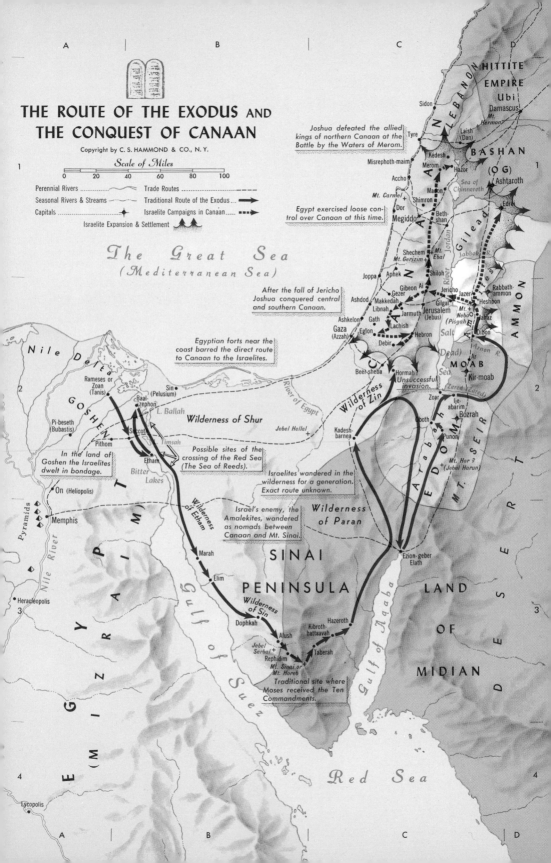

THE ROUTE OF THE EXODUS AND THE CONQUEST OF CANAAN

Copyright by C. S. Hammond & Co., N. Y.

Scale of Miles

0   20   40   60   80   100

Perennial Rivers ....
Seasonal Rivers & Streams ....
Capitals ....
Trade Routes ....
Traditional Route of the Exodus ....
Israelite Campaigns in Canaan ....
Israelite Expansion & Settlement ....

The Great Sea
(Mediterranean Sea)

Joshua defeated the allied kings of northern Canaan at the Battle by the Waters of Merom.

Egypt exercised loose control over Canaan at this time.

After the fall of Jericho Joshua conquered central and southern Canaan.

Egyptian forts near the coast barred the direct route to Canaan to the Israelites.

In the land of Goshen the Israelites dwelt in bondage.

Possible sites of the crossing of the Red Sea (The Sea of Reeds).

Israelites wandered in the wilderness for a generation. Exact route unknown.

Israel's enemy, the Amalekites, wandered as nomads between Canaan and Mt. Sinai.

Unsuccessful invasion.

Traditional site where Moses received the Ten Commandments.

HITTITE EMPIRE
Ubi
Damascus
Mt. Hermon?
BASHAN
(OG)
Ashtaroth
Edrei

Sidon
Tyre
Laish (Dan)
Kedesh
Merom
Misrephoth-maim
Hazor
Accho
Madon
Shimron
Sea of Chinnereth
Mt. Carmel
Dor
Megiddo
Bethshan
Gilead
Jabbok R.
Shechem
Mt. Ebal
Mt. Gerizim
Shiloh
Joppa
Aphek
Gezer
Gibeon Ai
Jericho
Jazer
Rabbath-ammon
AMMON
Ashdod
Makkedah
Gilgal
Heshbon
Libnah
Jerusalem (Jebus)
Mt. Nebo (Pisgah)
Jahaz
Ashkelon
Gath
Jarmuth
Lachish
Eglon
Hebron
Salt
Dibon
Gaza (Azzah)
Debir
(Dead)
Sea
MOAB
Beer-sheba
Hormah
Ar
Kir-moab
Zered Y. Zered
Zoar
Ije-abarim
Bozrah
Kadesh-barnea
Oboth
Punon
Mt. Hor? (Jebel Harun)
EDOM
MT. SEIR

Nile Delta

Rameses or Zoan (Tanis)
Sin (Pelusium)
Baal-zephon
L. Ballah
GOSHEN
Pi-beseth (Bubastis)
Succoth
Pithom
Wilderness of Shur
River of Egypt
Jebel Hellal
Etham
Timsah
Bitter Lakes
On (Heliopolis)
Wilderness of Etham
Pyramids
Memphis
Marah
Wilderness of Zin
Wilderness of Paran
Elim
Ezion-geber Elath
SINAI PENINSULA
Heracleopolis
Wilderness of Sin
Dophkah
Hazeroth
Kibroth-hattaavah
Alush
Taberah
Jebel Serbal
Rephidim
Mt. Sinai or Mt. Horeb
LAND OF MIDIAN
Gulf of Suez
Gulf of Aqaba
DESERT
Lycopolis
Nile River
EGYPT (MIZRAIM)
CANAAN
Arabah

Red Sea

Only rebel not ye against the Lord, neither fear ye
the people of the land; for they are bread for us: their
defence is departed from them, and the Lord is with us:
fear them not.[9]

And thus, upon this most important occasion, Moses
had called all the Israelites together in conference and as
instructed by the Lord, appointed Joshua to be their leader
and prophet, conferring this authority by the laying on
of hands.

Moses Preserved from Death

The Old Testament scriptures say that Moses died and
was buried, but we know that Moses was translated and
was not buried. The scriptures even identify the tomb
where he was buried, but in the light of modern revelation this is not true. Moses had to live in order to give the
keys of the gathering of Israel, which could not be trans-
mitted unless he was still able to do it through the flesh,
the same as Elijah, who was translated for the same purpose, with regard to the transmissal and conferring of the
keys which he held.

From that we understand why Elijah and Moses were
preserved from death—because they had a mission to per-
form, and it had to be performed before the crucifixion
of the Son of God, and therefore it could not be done in
the spirit. They had to have tangible bodies.[10]

Moses Reminds the Youth of Israel

What Moses said to these young Israelites, as they
stood on the threshold of obtaining this prized heritage,
refers to one of the great events of the history of God's
dealings with his children here in this life and is one of
the great scripture lessons of the Old Testament.

These be the words which Moses spake unto all Israel
on this side Jordan in the wilderness, in the plain over

---

[9]Numbers 14:6-9.
[10]Joseph Fielding Smith, *Elijah the Prophet*, p. 28.

against the Red sea, between Paran, and Tophel, and
Laban, and Hazeroth, and Dizahab.

(There are eleven days' journey from Horeb by way
of mount Seir unto Kadesh-barnea.)[11]

Here they stood reminded that from Mount Sinai,
which was also called Horeb, it took only eleven days by
camel train going along the base of the ridge of mountains
known as Mount Seir. The camel trains went along the
base of the mountains to avoid the heat of the desert and
it took them only eleven days to make the journey from
Horeb to Kadesh-barnea which was the gateway into the
promised land. Yet, it had taken Israel thirty-eight and
one-half years to travel that distance. (An automobile
could travel the same distance today in three hours, and
by plane it would take one hour.) Here was the great
lesson that Moses was impressing upon these young Israelites, not to make the mistake of those for whom the wanderings were necessary because they lacked the faith and
vision.

A Daily Application of this Lesson

If one wanted to make application of that story, the
same is true in people's lives. Many times it takes us a
whole lifetime to learn the lessons that we could learn in
but a few minutes because we lack the faith and the desire
to serve the Lord singly. Many times we go through hard-
ships and sorrows the same as the children of Israel did
because we lack the faith to do what the Lord wanted us
to do in the first place.

The Importance of the House of Israel

These twelve tribes of people that had gone into
Egypt, as revealed to us in the scriptural accounts, (Genesis 46) constituted the descendants of the twelve princes
of Israel, and these twelve princes of Israel had as their
progenitors, in addition to Israel or Jacob, Isaac, the father
of Jacob, and Abraham the father of Isaac. The house of
Israel sired by these great progenitors holds a very im-

---

[11]Deut. 1:1-2.

The remains of the walls of the Canaanite fortress of Jericho.

portant place in the plan of the gospel, as it has been revealed and is taught by the Church.

Members of the Church of Jesus Christ of Latter-day
Saints know of the importance of the house of Israel, and
its relationship to the plan of the gospel, and having been
baptized and had hands laid upon their heads for the receiving of the Holy Ghost, can have these things brought
to their remembrance that they may know what the Lord
has in store for his chosen people. The house of Israel
represents the chosen children of God. There *is* a chosen
people—there *is* a royal lineage that exists here upon the
earth, born unto it by virtue of their pre-existent worthiness. Some further explanation of this will follow. But
first, reference is made to several scriptures in both the
Old and New Testaments which will indicate this point
scripturally.

> But ye are a chosen generation, a royal priesthood,
> an holy nation, a peculiar people; that ye should shew forth
> the praises of him who hath called you out of darkness
> into his marvellous light.[12]

And then in contemplation of the fulfilment of their
foreordained nobility, God spoke unto ancient Israel,

> Now therefore, if ye will obey my voice indeed, and
> keep my covenant, then ye shall be a peculiar treasure
> unto me above all people: for all the earth is mine:
> And ye shall be unto me a kingdom of priests, and an
> holy nation. These are the words which thou shalt speak
> unto the children of Israel.[13]

Of the great prophet Abraham, God announced his
pre-existent worthiness and foreordained calling for this
life and the one to follow.

> Now the Lord had shown unto me, Abraham, the
> intelligences that were organized before the world was;
> and among all these there were many of the noble and
> great ones;

---

[12]1 Peter 2:9.
[13]Exodus 19:5-6.

And God saw these souls that they were good, and
he stood in the midst of them, and he said: These I will
make my rulers; for he stood among those that were
spirits, and he saw that they were good; and he said unto
me: Abraham, thou art one of them; thou wast chosen
before thou wast born.[14]

The Lord told of knowing Jeremiah before mortal
birth.

Before I formed thee in the belly I knew thee; and
before thou camest forth out of the womb I sanctified
thee, and I ordained thee a prophet unto the nations.[15]

From the same book of Deuteronomy in the Old Testament, which contains the instructions that Moses gave
to this vast gathering of people, who were then waiting
to go into the promised land, which they later took by
conquest under the leadership of Joshua, we learn of the
further instructions given which reminded them of their
noble lineage and position as a chosen people of God.

Remember the days of old, consider the years of
many generations: ask thy father, and he will shew thee;
thy elders, and they will tell thee.

The manner in which Moses spoke indicated that what
he said was common knowledge among the children of
Israel at that time. Continuing he said,

When the Most High divided to the nations their
inheritance, when he separated the sons of Adam, he
set the bounds of the people according to the number
of the children of Israel.[16]

This is a very important scripture to remember. From
it we learn that the very boundaries of every nation that
has ever existed in this world are determined as to its
length of time, as to its inhabitants and its opportunity
to receive the gospel, by the number of the children of

---

[14]P. of G. P., Abraham 3:22-23.
[15]Jeremiah 1:5.
[16]Deut. 32:7-8.

noble lineage that are born unto mortal probation in that particular nation. This is why the blood of Israel is sprinkled throughout all of the earth, the purpose of which is to serve the great plan of life and salvation, in providing every nation, kindred, tongue, and people the right to hear the message of the plan of life and salvation and through the leaven that leaveneth the lump be amenable to its acceptance.

Using these scriptures as a beginning and continuing with the enlightenment that comes from revelation received through Joseph Smith, these thoughts are pursued further.

An important scripture from the Pearl of Great Price is quoted with some comments on what the conditions were that existed in the pre-existence with regard to each spirit child of God that lived there. This mortal life is not the beginning nor the end of our existence; it is an interlude, an interim period, actually a probation, a connection between the life before and the life after mortality. It is very, very short even at longest, and yet, how very important it is, in relationship to the entire eternity of man's existence. Since mortality is but a continuation of that life before, it is vital that we understand the pre-existence. Then, if we are to understand the pre-existence and its purposes, we must also understand that period or estate subsequent to this life. Mortality as a continuing part of man's existence, therefore, becomes increasingly important as you think of it in the sense of eternity rather than just the few short years spent in this life. From the Pearl of Great Price are found these words of the Lord unto Abraham:

> And the Lord said unto me: These two facts do exist, that there are two spirits, one being more intelligent than the other; there shall be another more intelligent than they; I am the Lord thy God, I am more intelligent than they all.[17]

---

[17]P. of G. P., Abraham 3:19.

This scripture reveals clearly to us that in the pre-existence there were three divisions of people, and within these general divisions there were undoubtedly further gradations. I repeat, these two facts exist, that where there are *two* spirits, one is more intelligent than the other. There is still *another* more intelligent than these two, but the Lord God is more intelligent than these three. Categorically, we find from this scripture that the spirits of individuals in the pre-existence were graded as to their status of development in all its required phases. Thus in the pre-existence, exercising our free agency, we all developed in varying degrees from previous spheres where we existed as intelligences.

The Spirit Body

In the spirit world we received our spirit body of which the physical body is the exact image. When we were intelligences without a spiritual body, we must have also had free agency, for we also developed there. When we emerged from that period to receive a spiritual body, there was no doubt a judgment placed upon us and assignments made whereby in accordance with the kind of persons we were, and by the standard of our obedience there, we became members of or developed into, in varying degrees, one of these three divisions of people that existed in the pre-existence, classified as the Lord designated unto Abraham. Hence there were three general divisions of spirits, one more intelligent than the other, and the third more intelligent than they, and God more intelligent than them all.

When the earth was planned, in order to have all these spirits born into a probationary period, or the second estate, it was necessary to follow a plan of procreation. By that is meant the plan by which both male and female would be born into this life. This must obviously be a part of the plan of salvation. The very nature of each person, therefore, would require that their birth would fit the caliber of their person; this, no doubt, entailed a birth into mortality by pre-existent judgment. Equality of birth could not be possible, because there is no equality of spirit persons. Thus to bring about birth into mortality there must have been a need to preserve the station to which each one had developed in the pre-existence. This can be explained further by referring again to the revelation from the Lord to Abraham.

> Now the Lord had shown unto me, Abraham, the intelligences that were organized before the world was; and among all these there were many of the noble and great ones;
>
> And God saw these souls that they were good, and he stood in the midst of them, and he said: These I will make my rulers; for he stood among those that were spirits, and he saw that they were good; and he said unto me: Abraham, thou art one of them; thou wast chosen before thou wast born.[18]

And the consequence of this was, that in order for man to come into this life, there needed to be a judgment, just the same as there will ultimately be a judgment when we leave this life and prepare to enter our final stations of existence in the next estate. Every time we enter an estate there is apparently a judgment, and people are placed in the category or division to which they rightfully belong.

The Peopling of the Earth

Now let us go to the beginning of the peopling of the earth. When Adam and Eve were placed in the Garden of Eden in order to bring about a fall, they had to deliberately do this of their own volition. This is why the scriptures tell us clearly that Adam was not deceived. Adam had to submit to the fall of his own free will. It could not be thrust upon him. Adam was not deceived; the woman was deceived; but Adam was not deceived.

> And Adam was not deceived, but the woman being deceived was in the transgression.[19]

As stated, had he been deceived, he could not have brought about the fall. This, of necessity, was the product

---

[18]*Ibid.*, 3:22-23.
[19]1 Timothy 2:14.

of the exercise of agency, and the same thing was true of
Christ when he accomplished the atoning sacrifice.

> No man taketh it from me, but I lay it down of myself.
> I have power to lay it down, and I have power to take
> it again.   This commandment have I received of my
> Father.[20]

He had the power to resist death, but he voluntarily
gave his life so that he could bring about the atonement
by the laws and principles of free agency. And though
we do not understand fully how the fall and the atonement
are actually effected, we, nevertheless, accept as an important part of our faith the efficacy of these two acts
necessary to our salvation.

Thus when Adam and Eve, because of their deliberate
willingness to do what they did, and especially in the case
of Adam, partook of the fruit, something happened in their
bodies that caused a deterioration, and they became mortal
and as such their offspring would be mortal.

> And Adam knew his wife, and she bare unto him sons
> and daughters, and they began to multiply and to replenish
> the earth.[21]

Adam and Eve through the process of the fall thus
commenced the multiplying and replenishing of the earth
by bringing into the world by mortal birth the vast con-
course of spirits who waited in the three pre-existent divisions to be born into this mortal probation.

> And in that day the Holy Ghost fell upon Adam,
> which beareth record of the Father and the Son, saying:
> I am the Only Begotten of the Father from the beginning,
> henceforth and forever, that as thou hast fallen thou
> mayest be redeemed, and all mankind, even as many as
> will.[22]

Born unto Adam and Eve was Cain, and Cain no
doubt was a spirit of a lower kingdom or division of the

---

[20]John 10:18.
[21]P. of G. P., Moses 5:2.
[22]*Ibid.*, 5:9.

pre-existence. In the processes of earth life obedience to the gospel, necessary to return to God's presence, he would not follow the priesthood and the counsel with it, even though the Lord said unto him,

> . . . Cain: Why art thou wroth? Why is thy countenance fallen?
>
> If thou doest well, thou shalt be accepted.[23]

But he rejected the Lord's counsel, and rebelled against the priesthood of God and was cursed. And thus through the lineage of Cain henceforth were to be born those spirits who had received a lesser appointment in the pre-existence, where undoubtedly they had rejected the priesthood also. Of this we read in the *Journal of Discourses,*

> Why are so many of the inhabitants of the earth cursed with a skin of blackness? It comes in consequence of their fathers rejecting the power of the Holy Priesthood and the law of God. They will go down to death. And when all the rest of the children have received their blessings in the Holy Priesthood, and they will then come up and possess the priesthood, and receive all the blessings.[24]

The birth into mortality is not a matter of chance occurrence or of uncalculated purpose. All is in accordance with a plan. Those who are in the lower division in the pre-existence are born into this life in a lower division, where the normal condition of their place has that encumbrance fitted to their own worthiness. Those who were in the less valiant division will be born into the less valiant division. Those who were the noble ones, such as Abraham and such as all those who receive the priesthood in this life, were generally of the higher division; and consequently, they are born into such channels as will preserve their place that they held in the pre-existence, and of

---

[23]*Ibid.,* 5:22-23.
[24]*Journal of Discourses,* Vol. III, p. 272.

which they have received a judgment in the station of
their mortal birth. (See quotation on page 171 of this
article.)

With this explanation, the reason can be seen why it is
that we have different kinds of people upon the earth, why
it is that we have cursed lineages and retarded civilizations
all over the world, although, as stated, within these there
are varying degrees. For example, in the northern part of
India there is a rapidly diminishing people known as the
Weddas. Had your spirit been born among them, your
whole mortal life would have transpired in less than 21
years. Sixty percent of these people die before they reach
the age of one. If you were fortunate enough to live a
full 21 years, you would have had little or no memory.
They can count only up to three or four and that by visual
perception. They have only a few vocables in order to
make themselves known. Now, ask yourself the question,
why were you not born among these people? And then
follow **the question and ask yourself** why you were not
born to other lineages and be restricted in receiving of the
priesthood of God? Why were you born as you are? Why
were you born to have access to the gospel of Jesus Christ?
With these questions you begin to understand that in the
distribution of mankind as spirits are born into this life,
there exist gradations, or distinct divisions of people.

The Parable of the Talents

In one of the last parables that the Lord related before
his crucifixion, a parable, it is feared, that is often misued
and the extent of its true meaning lost, for it is said by some
that the parable of the talents has to do with our educa-
tional, cultural, musical, or other personal traits or achievement. This does not seem to fit the pertinent fact of its
intended meaning. The Lord, I believe, is not referring
to that. He speaks, rather, of the divisions of mankind,
and of our stations in life. The two key scriptures in this
parable are most informative.

> For the kingdom of heaven is as a man travelling into a far country, who called his own servants, and delivered unto them his goods.
>
> And unto one he gave *five talents.*

(In other words, I believe if you interpret this correctly, unto those people who were of the higher lineage in the pre-existence, he gave five talents.)

> . . . to *another two.*

(Another of this station refers to those who were not so valiant, but still who did not rebel against the plan of the gospel in the pre-existence, and thus merited, in the main, birth into this life in the graded second division and will leave it, unless full acceptance of the gospel is achieved, heirs only of the terrestrial kingdom. And ultimately as such they will not receive of the fulness of the gospel plan, and though they may acknowledge it in the spirit world, it will not be to their higher glorification.)

> And to *another one.*

(Represented by the lesser division of mankind, or the people who may never receive the fulness of the gospel and are heirs of the lesser or telestial kingdom.) Then the Lord says that after he had given these, he took his journey and left.

Verses 31 and 32 reveal the key to the Master's words.

> When the Son of man shall come in his glory, and all the holy angels with him, then shall he sit upon the throne of his glory:
>
> And before him shall be gathered *all nations*: and he shall *separate them one from another,* . . .[25]

This, therefore, suggests a meaning of the parable of the talents.

The Sons of Men—the Sons of God

As the children of Cain increased they were known as sons and daughters of men. The scriptures tell us simply,

---

[25]Matthew 25:14, 15, 31-32.

that the sons of God married the daughters of men, and the daughters of God married the sons of men. While the sons and daughters of God adhered to the covenant which God gave to Adam and accepted the priesthood, the sons and daughters of men followed Lucifer and were deceived. It is presumed that there were so many sons of God marrying daughters of men, or vice versa, that it became necessary to destroy the earth by flood. The suggested meaning of this is that the procreation of the spirit children from the pre-existence was getting out of balance, with its attendant wickedness, requiring a new beginning and repopulation of the earth. Undoubtedly foreordained as such, yet its implied purpose is very real.

Noah and Three Sons

It is to be pondered why it was that Noah had only three sons with him in the ark of the flood. Why didn't he have four? Could it have been the will of the Lord that he have three? And these three sons of the great patriarch Noah became the principal progenitors of mankind in this life, although Adam, through his sons, had been the original progenitor.

But with the destruction of all mankind by the flood, except Noah and his three sons and their wives, the peopling of earth began all over aagin. Japheth, Shem, and Ham obviously, therefore, became the sires of the races or civilizations of mankind that exist upon the earth today; they have preserved through their lineages, the three divisions of man, which obtained in the pre-existence and which then as now have its counterpart for procreation here in mortality.

Shem

Shem, although not the eldest, was placed above Japheth and thus received the birthright. Through the lineage of Shem have come and will continue to come the chosen spirits of the pre-existence, those who were noble ones such as Abraham, for the Lord had said unto Abraham,

"Thou wast one of them." These have been born into mortality through this lineage.

Japheth

Japheth was given the second place, and through him has been born and will yet be born the lineage of people that were classified in the second division of men and these we call the lineage of adoption or the gentile. (The Jewish interpretation of the gentile cannot be the logical one as it is applied in this broad sense. According to our knowledge of the gospel, a gentile is a descendant of Japheth.) (See Genesis ch. 10.)

Ham

Through the lineage of Ham and the descendancy of Phut have come the colored or black races.

Ethnologically it is not too difficult to trace the races or civilizations of mankind as they have come down the stream of time. (This is a separate study but a most interesting one.)

The covenants which Noah made with his three children, are most important, a knowledge of which is significant to an understanding of the overall plan of the gospel.

Ham Rejects Noah and the Priesthood

The ninth chapter of Genesis, in obvious legendary fashion, states that Noah became drunken on wine and lay in his tent naked, and when Ham came in he made fun of his father and when Japheth and Shem heard of it, they went into the tent backward with a covering and placed the covering over their father out of respect for him. They then rebuked their brother Ham because he had failed to recognize the honor and dignity of his own father. This apparent Jewish story served to convey the lesson of its writing. It was a way of telling how Ham had not respected the priesthood of Noah and was consequently denied it. We are instructed in this important happening from the writings of Abraham.

Now this king of Egypt was a descendant from the loins of Ham, and was a partaker of the blood of the Canaanites by birth.

From this descent sprang all the Egyptians, and thus the blood of the Canaanites was preserved in the land.

The land of Egypt being first discovered by a woman, who was the daughter of Ham, and the daughter of Egyptus, which in the Chaldean signifies Egypt, which signifies that which is forbidden.

When this woman discovered the land it was under water, who afterward settled her sons in it; and thus, from Ham, sprang that race which preserved the curse in the land.

Now the first government of Egypt was established by Pharoah, the eldest son of Egyptus, the daughter of Ham, and it was after the manner of the government of Ham, which was patriarchal.

Pharaoh, being a righteous man, established his kingdom and judged his people wisely and justly all his days, seeking earnestly to *imitate* that order established by the fathers in the first generations, in the days of the first patriarchal reign, even in the reign of Adam, and also of Noah, his father, who blessed him with the blessings of the earth, and with the blessings of wisdom, *but cursed him as pertaining to the Priesthood.*

Now, Pharaoh being of that lineage by which he could not have the right of Priesthood, notwithstanding the Pharaohs would fain claim it from Noah, through Ham. . . .[26]

Thus we observe with Ham a similar experience of priesthood rejection which had occurred with Cain. And, therefore, the lineage of birth of the cursed people is preserved through Ham, one of the sons of Noah. Japheth and Shem are depicted as respecting their father Noah and the priesthood. Shem, for some reason, was more valiant in his acceptance of it than was Japheth, the result of which was that Shem received the birthright over his brother Japheth. Nevertheless when Noah made the covenants with his three sons, which is a patriarchal custom, the important blessings and covenants were bestowed upon Shem and Japheth, though Ham was blessed as a servant and as such

---

[26]P. of G. P., Abraham 1:21-27.

in due time, would receive certain blessings of the household of Shem, or literally Israel, as was the custom in all ancient patriarchal families. We learn of this in the ninth chapter of Genesis.

> And Noah awoke from his wine, and knew what his younger son had done unto him. (Continuing the allegory that the Jewish people used),
> And he said, Cursed be Canaan; a servant of servants shall he be unto his brethren.[27]

This is not speaking about an individual, but rather about a race of people.

Unto Shem he said:

> Blessed be the Lord God of Shem; and Canaan shall be his servant.[28]

In the blessings which Noah continued to bestow upon his sons there followed a marvelous promise unto Japheth which is emphasized.

> God shall enlarge Japheth, and he shall dwell in the tents of Shem; . . .[29]

In other words, God shall enlarge Japheth and provide for him and his descendants the opportunity to come in and dwell in the tents of Shem, or the house of the descendants of Shem, or the house of Israel, for truly the house of Israel is descendant from Shem. Thus the covenant was made unto Japheth and his descendant civilizations, that in the progress of life he would receive this great opportunity to raise his station of existence in the eternal plan.

A Commencement of a Work

It must surely be known to all that we are proclaiming the gospel of Jesus Christ principally unto the gentile at this time. This is the day of the gentile. Yes, today. The day of the Lamanite has not yet fully come, nor of the Jew, nor of the cursed lineages; the day for them will not

---

[27]Genesis 9:24-25.
[28]Ibid., 9:26.
[29]Ibid., 9:27.

come until after the city of the New Jerusalem is built,
and the temple of God will be erected in Jackson County,
Missouri. And although some preliminary work of teaching
the gospel to these factions may have started, in that day,
together with their redemption will come the full restoration of the other tribes of Israel and all of God's children
who will respond to the gathering call. The ten tribes will
also be led from their hiding place to the city of the New
Jerusalem, as proclaimed by the Lord to the Nephites.

> And then shall the work of the Father commence at
> that day, even when this gospel shall be preached among
> the remnant of this people. Verily I say unto you, at that
> day shall the work of the Father commence among all the
> dispersed of my people, yea, even the tribes which have
> been lost, which the Father hath led away out of
> Jerusalem.
>
> Yea, the work shall commence among all the dis-
> persed of my people, with the Father, to prepare the way
> whereby they may come unto me, that they may call on
> the Father in my name.
>
> Yea, and then shall the work commence, with the
> Father, among all nations, in preparing the way whereby
> his people may be gathered home to the land of their
> inheritance.[30]

The Leadership of the Tribe of Ephraim

But the Lord has sent one of the tribes ahead to prepare the way for the coming of the other tribes. All who
join the Church today, with few exceptions, are of, or
assigned to, the tribe of Ephraim.

It is significant to point out that Joshua, a descendant
of Ephraim (see Numbers 13:6-8), became the leader and
prophet of ancient Israel succeeding Moses.

> And the men, which Moses sent to search the land,
> who returned, and made all the congregation to murmur
> against him, by bringing up a slander upon the land,
>
> Even those men that did bring up the evil report
> upon the land, died by the plague before the Lord.

---

[30]3 Nephi 21:26-28.

> But Joshua the son of Nun, and Caleb the son of Jephunneh, which were of the men that went to search the land, lived still.[31]

Now, in the latter days, as the Lord begins the work to call his chosen house and people together, it is Ephraim, the captain of the house of Israel, who has the assignment to lead and prepare the way. Thus we witness by our own patriarchal blessings and designation of lineage, that primarily only those who are of and who are to be assigned to the tribe of Ephraim are being called, and this through the loins of Joseph, the chosen of Israel. Thus your patriarchal blessing confirms what is transpiring.

It would appear that those who will ultimately occupy the celestial kingdom will be those who will make up the twelve tribes of Israel, God's covenant people. And any who go into that kingdom, if they are not rightfully members of the twelve tribes by blood descent, will be assigned, by adoption, to one or another of the twelve tribes. But we also see, that the tribe of Ephraim is being called first, as it was announced anciently,

> . . . I am a father to Israel, and Ephraim is my first-born.[32]

The other tribes will be called in the proper time of the Lord. (See 3 Nephi ch. 21.)

The Day of the Gentile

The question may be rightfully asked at this point, "How does the covenant, which Noah made with his son, Japheth, through whose lineage have been born countless millions of middle division spirits of the pre-existence whom we refer to as gentiles and to whom the gospel may be taken, affect the missionary program of the Church today?"

To understand this more completely, reference is

---

[31]Numbers 14:36-38; see also 14:6.
[32]Jer. 31:9.

made to prophecies in the Book of Mormon. First from
1st Nephi:

> Wherefore, these things go forth from the Jews in
> purity unto the *Gentiles,* according to the truth which is
> in God.
>
> And after they go forth by the hand of the twelve
> apostles of the Lamb, from the Jews unto the Gentiles,
> thou seest the foundation of a great and abominable
> church, which is most abominable above all other churches;
> for behold, they have taken away from the gospel of the
> Lamb many parts which are plain and most precious; and
> also many covenants of the Lord have they taken away.
>
> And all this have they done that they might pervert
> the right ways of the Lord, that they might blind the
> eyes and harden the hearts of the children of men.
>
> Wherefore, thou seest that after the book hath gone
> forth through the hands of the great and abominable
> church, that there are many plain and precious things
> taken away from the book, which is the book of the
> Lamb of God.
>
> And after these plain and precious things were taken
> away it goeth forth unto *all the nations of the Gentiles;*
> and after it goeth forth unto all the nations of the Gentiles,
> yea, even across the many waters which thou hast seen
> with the Gentiles which have gone forth out of captivity,
> thou seest—because of the many plain and precious things
> which have been taken out of the book, which were plain
> unto the understanding of the children of men, according
> to the plainness which is in the Lamb of God—because of
> these things which are taken away out of the gospel of
> the Lamb, an exceeding great many do stumble, yea, inso-
> much that Satan hath great power over them.
>
> Nevertheless, thou beholdest that the Gentiles who
> have gone forth out of captivity, and have been lifted
> up by the power of God above all other nations, upon
> the face of the land which is choice above all other lands
> [North and South America], which is the land that the
> Lord God hath covenanted with thy father that his seed
> should have for the land of their inheritance; wherefore,
> thou seest that the Lord God will not suffer that the
> Gentiles will utterly destroy the mixture of thy seed, which
> are among thy brethren.[33]

---

[33] 1 Nephi 13:25-30.

And then from the fourteenth chapter:

> And it shall come to pass, that if the Gentiles shall hearken unto the Lamb of God in that day that he shall manifest himself unto them in word, and also in power, in very deed, *unto the taking away of their stumbling blocks—*
>
> And harden not their hearts against the Lamb of God, they shall be numbered among the seed of thy father; *yea, they shall be numbered among the house of Israel....*[34]

Herein the Lord identifies the period of time in which we are now living, by his words which tell also of the coming forth of the Bible. The King James version of the New and Old Testaments, which we accept as a Church as being the most accurate, was published during the seventeenth century, and this version, more nearly correct than others, still is not complete, nor do we accept in all instances its literal translation. The modern versions of the Bible, which are gaining in popularity principally among the modern sectarian clergy, are even further from full acceptance by the Church. One of our Articles of Faith clarifies our stand in this regard.

> We believe the Bible to be the word of God as far as it is translated correctly; . . .[35]

With regard to the taking of the gospel to the gentiles, the Lord, through Nephi, had this to say further, found in 3rd Nephi, identifying again the particular day in which we now live.

> And verily I say unto you, I give unto you a sign, that ye may know the time when these things shall be about to take place—that I shall gather in, from their long dispersion, my people, O house of Israel, and shall establish again among them my Zion; . . .
>
> For thus it behooveth the Father that it should come forth from the Gentiles, that he may show forth his power unto the Gentiles, for this cause that the Gentiles,

---

[34]*Ibid.*, 14:1-2.
[35]Eighth Article of Faith.

if they will not harden their hearts, that they may repent
and come unto me and be baptized in my name and know
of the true points of my doctrine, that they may be numbered among my people, O house of Israel.[36]

This, of course, refers to the gentiles, for the Lord,
during his ministry among the Nephites made known unto
them as quoted, what would take place in the last days, as
he unfolded the plan of carrying the gospel unto the gentiles. To amplify this period of time, known as "the day of
the gentile," the Lord spoke further unto the Nephites of
the coming forth of the gospel, and he told them that a
man would declare it unto them, (Joseph Smith) whom
they for the most part would not believe. I refer to the
words of the Lord found in 3 Nephi:

> For in that day, for my sake shall the Father work
> a work, which shall be a great and a marvelous work
> among them; and there shall be among them those who
> will not believe it, although a man shall declare it unto
> them.
>
> But behold, the life of my servant shall be in my
> hand; therefore they shall not hurt him, although he shall
> be marred because of them. Yet I will heal him, for I will
> show unto them that my wisdom is greater than the
> cunning of the devil.
>
> Therefore it shall come to pass that whosoever will
> not believe in my words, who am Jesus Christ, which the
> Father shall cause him to bring forth unto the Gentiles,
> and shall give unto him power that he shall bring them
> forth unto the Gentiles, (it shall be done even as Moses
> said) they shall be cut off from among my people who
> are of the covenant.[37]

Now, actually, we are witnessing the fulfilment of this
prophetic period, as the gospel is taken to the gentiles.
This is their last opportunity to receive it. If the people
of the lands of Europe and elsewhere, where the gentile
races reside, do not receive the gospel now, judgments
and disasters will happen, that what has gone on before
among them will be nothing in comparison. For when

---

[36]3 Nephi 21:1, 6.
[37]Ibid., 9-11.

the Lord withdraws his Spirit from these lands, there will be great destruction and suffering. We think of the terror that has already happened throughout the world, but this is nothing compared to that which the Lord will permit if the gentiles fail now to repent—theirs is a great promise. Here is the further statement of the Lord on this:

> For it shall come to pass, saith the Father, that at that day whosoever will not repent and come unto my Beloved Son, them will I cut off from among my people, O house of Israel;
>
> And I will execute vengeance and fury upon them, even as upon the heathen, such as they have not heard.
>
> But if they will repent and hearken unto my words, and harden not their hearts, I will establish my church among them, and they shall come in unto the covenant and be numbered among this the remnant of Jacob, unto whom I have given this land for their inheritance;
>
> And they shall assist my people, the remnant of Jacob, and also as many of the house of Israel as shall come, that they may build a city, which shall be called the New Jerusalem.[38]

But if they will repent and hearken unto the Lord, and harden not their hearts, his Church will be established among them, and they shall come in and be numbered among the house of Israel, together with the remnant of the seed, or the Lamanites. Here then is the promise and prophecy from the Lord. These things must transpire. It is the plan of the gospel; it will go forth as the heralds of truth proclaim it unto the gentile nations.

The Lord in these prophecies speaks more generally of the gentiles who will occupy the promised land of America. But the proclaiming of the gospel unto the gentile is not confined by prophecy to those in America as explained by 1st Nephi.

> And after these plain and precious things were taken away it goeth forth *unto all the nations of the Gentiles;* and after it goeth forth *unto all the nations of the Gentiles,*

---

[38]*Ibid.*, 21:20-23.

yea, even across the many waters which thou hast seen
with the Gentiles which have gone forth out of captivity,
thou seest—because of the many plain and precious things
which have been taken out of the book, which were plain
unto the understanding of the children of men, according
to the plainness which is in the Lamb of God—because of
these things which are taken away out of the gospel of
the Lamb, an exceeding great many do stumble, yea,
insomuch that Satan hath great power over them.[39]

Who then are the gentile nations? The tenth chapter of
Genesis reveals the genealogy of the children of Japheth,
the eldest son of Noah. They are not too difficult to
trace, even today, with their many migrations and civilizations. Two excellent sources of information on the ethnology of Japheth can be found in the *Races of Mankind*
by Ridpath, and the *Origin of Nations* by Rawlinson. The
latter in particular will prove most enlightening, not only
as to the descendants of Japheth, but will also pronounce
quite clearly who the descendants of all the three sons of
Noah really are.

The tenth chapter of Genesis in the Old Testament
provides the key in determining the ancestry of these gentile nations. Often the Old Testament is neglected in our
search for the truth but this should not be so. This chapter
is probably one of the most important in all of the Holy
Bible so far as its implied effect upon the human race in
this particular dispensation is concerned.

It outlines the ancient genealogy of peoples and provides the source, that we may today learn who the descendants of the three sons of Noah are. As these gentile
progenitors are identified it becomes evident that the historical writers of this important record are not telling of
individuals but are rather referring ethnologically to races
or civilizations. A part of this record as it refers to the
descendants of Japheth is quoted:

Now these are the generations of the sons of Noah,
Shem, Ham, and Japheth: and unto them were sons born
after the flood.

---

[39]1 Nephi 13:29.

The sons of Japheth; Gomer, and Magog, and Madai, and Javan, and Tubal, and Meshech, and Tiras.

And the sons of Gomer; Ashkenaz, and Riphath, and Togarmah.

And the sons of Javan; Elishah, and Tarshish, Kittim, and Dodanim.

By these were the isles of the Gentiles divided in their lands; every one after his tongue, after their families, in their nations.[40]

Without going into detail let us attempt to identify some of the descendants of the anciently recorded races who came from Japheth, the eldest son of Noah, and concerning whom a covenant was made with by Noah leading to their inclusion in the house of Israel, if faithful and obedient to the gospel, in the day of the gentile which day is *today*.

The Descendant Civilizations of Japheth

Briefly then, the descendants of Gomer are the French and the British. Those of Magog are the Germans and the Slavs. Of Madai are those people in the Far and Middle East principally the Hindu, the Korean, and the Japanese, and those of the Malayan Peninsula. These people are all descendants through eastern migrations from Madai who formed a civilization descendant from Japheth. Then we have Javan who is the ancestor of the people of Greece and Turkey and of the inland countries to whom we are not permitted to carry the gospel as yet. Then we have Tubal, not so clearly identified, but no doubt of Spain, Italy, and the Near East. Lastly, of Tiras and Meshech; these find their ethnic affinities in Siberia and Russia. The many references to rivers, mountains, customs, writings, and other things connect civilization with civilization which in the earlier days settled first in the nearby areas of Egypt, Palestine, and the Near East, then by migration into extended areas throughout what is now modern Europe and Asia, and provides almost certain information as

----

[40]Genesis 10:1-5.

these descendancies are traced to our modern time, bringing to us the reality that we are actually proclaiming the gospel to the descendants of Japheth and are thus fulfilling the covenant of Noah unto him.

The Blood of Israel

But, also in accordance with ancient covenants, particularly the one made with Abraham, concerning the blessing of all people through his lineage, meaning of Israel, which is quoted in Genesis:

> And in thy seed shall all the nations of the earth be blessed; because thou hast obeyed my voice.[41]

The blood of Israel, particularly that of Ephraim, has been sprinkled among these very nations. The Prophet Joseph Smith was a blood descendant of Ephraim. It is difficult for members of the Church to know how much of the blood of Ephraim they have in their bodies, although a designated member of that tribe. But it is almost a sure thing that a great deal of gentile blood is in all who accept the gospel, mixed as it may well be with the blood of Ephraim. But it matters not for when converts accept the gospel from among these gentile nations today, they are assigned to the tribe of Ephraim, almost without exception. The characteristic of gentiles or those of the chosen seed when accepting the gospel are referred to in this writing of the Prophet Joseph Smith.

> There are two comforters spoken of. One is the Holy Ghost, the same as given on the day of Pentecost, and that all Saints receive after faith, repentance, and baptism. This first Comforter or Holy Ghost has no other effect than pure intelligence. It is more powerful in expanding the mind, enlightening the understanding, and storing the intellect with present knowledge, of a man who is *of the literal seed of Abraham,* than one that is a Gentile, though it may not have half as much visible effect upon the body; for as the Holy Ghost falls upon one of the literal seed of Abraham, *it is calm and serene;* and his whole soul and

---

[41]*Ibid.,* 22:18.

body are only exercised by the pure spirit of intelligence;
while the effect of the Holy Ghost upon a Gentile, *is to
purge out the old blood, and make him actually of the seed
of Abraham.* That man that has none of the blood of Abraham (naturally) must have a new creation by the Holy
Ghost. In such a case, there may be more of a powerful
effect upon the body, and visible to the eye, than upon
an Israelite, while the Israelite at first might be far before
the Gentile in pure intelligence.[42]

This is the duty of the gentile! And we are proclaiming the gospel unto them, and they are the vast number of
spirits that have come into the world assigned by birth to
the second division, but who undoubtedly were not valiant
in the pre-existence although they did not rebel against
God. We have them in the Church by the thousands, not
always valiant, accepting only that part of the gospel to
which they are attached for one reason or another. They
never rebel against anybody. They don't always pay a full
tithing, but they do their best. . . . they pay five percent,
and they don't always pay a full fast offering, but they
always pay some. They are probably guilty of the sin of
omission rather than the sin of commission; they are not
valiant in the testimony of the Lord. True valiance means
to sustain the Church and all of its teachings—not to select
just certain of its laws to keep, but to accept and obey all
of them.

There was also the lower division who rejected the
priesthood of God in the pre-existence and that is why
there are the cursed lineages. Some have said that they
were neutral in the pre-existence. I'm sure you have heard
that story. Well, this doesn't hold up with the revelations
or the teachings of the brethren. The Prophet Joseph Smith
states that the reason people are born colored and are under the restriction of not receiving the priesthood, at least
for the present, is caused by their rejection of the priesthood in the pre-existence. How, it may be asked, could
they have rejected the priesthood and were still not ban-

---

[42]*Teachings of the Prophet Joseph Smith,* (Joseph Fielding Smith) pp.
149-150.

ished with Lucifer, thus being permitted to stay in the
presence of God and be born into this life of probation,
although to a lower division? Revelation may provide
some light on this.

> And there was war in heaven: Michael and his angels
> fought against the dragon; and the dragon fought and his
> angels,
>
> And prevailed not; neither was their place found any
> more in heaven.
>
> And the great dragon was cast out, that old serpent,
> called the Devil, and Satan, which deceiveth the whole
> world: he was cast out into the earth, and his angels were
> cast out with him.[43]

Many have wondered why they were cast out upon
the earth. Perhaps until the final judgment there was no
other place for them to go. It would seem that their final
place of abode, although being prepared for them, their
consignment will not be until the end of the judgment of
this life. Consequently, there is no other place they could
reside for the present, than here upon the earth; they could
not remain in the presence of God because of their rebellion. Concerning their banishment, we read the following
scripture:

> And I heard a loud voice saying in heaven, Now is
> come salvation, and strength, and the kingdom of our God,
> and the power of his Christ: for the accuser of our brethren
> is cast down, which accused them before our God day and
> night.[44]

From this we learn somewhat of the difference between those of the lesser kingdom that came into the earth
in a lower division, while the sons of perdition were denied
the privileges of mortality and of the realm of preparation
for mortal birth. Though rejecting the priesthood, the former apparently did not lose the condition of potential
repentance, and thus the probation of earth life could have

---

[43]Rev. 12:7-9.
[44]*Ibid.*, 12:10.

effect upon them. Lucifer and the disobedient spirits that followed him—entirely without the capability of repentance and were thus outside of the gospel plan—manifested this awful condition by organizing a resistance against God and fought against him. He accused God; he accused Christ; and he did everything in his power to undermine the coming forth of this plan of salvation here upon the earth, and those who followed him supported this action.

The Mark of Apostasy

You can always tell a deep-rooted apostate in the Church today, and I have seen some of them, for after they are excommunicated they set to work to destroy the Church. That is precisely what David Whitmer did and many of the early-day leaders who, when they were cut off from the Church, organized a plan to undermine the Church. Because of this their ultimate fate is precarious. Had they just said, "We've made a mistake; Mormonism is false; and we want no part of it," and gone back to their farms and did no more, their condemnation would not be so great. In our own time we are able to witness something of the difference between a son of perdition and one who just rebels as it was in the pre-existence. Undoubtedly the distinguishing characteristic is summed up in one still having the power to repent while the other had not this power.

Sent Forth to Proclaim the Gospel to the Gentile

We send missionaries all over the world, and while we rejoice with our wonderful converts who join the Church, remember, we have only about 1,700,000 members. That isn't as many people as there are in the city of Berlin, Germany. There is nothing in the scriptures that indicates that we will go out and convert the world. The scriptures say, ". . . strait is the gate, and narrow is the way, . . . and few there be that find it."[45] And the Lord said unto his disciples on the Mount of Olives that "I will cut

---

[45]Matthew 7:14.

my work short lest even the very elect will be deceived."
In view of this, what then is our real purpose in testifying
and warning the people? This is to be remembered, because it gives some reason and purpose to the proclaiming
of the gospel of Jesus Christ, other than goals, and personal missionary satisfaction. We are assisting our Heavenly Father to gather from those in mortality the chosen
spirits of the pre-existence, and the spirits of adoption who
will valiantly accept the gospel in this life and prepare for
leadership in God's plan in readiness to assist in the governing and ruling all of God's children who will be assigned
to the three degrees of glory in the next estate.

The Doctrine and Covenants, Section 76, tells clearly
of the assignment of those of the priesthood to become
kings and priests, and in the full context of its meaning
refers to a condition after this life.

This is just another way of describing a condition of
leadership and of being an administrator in God's plan.
The ancient term of king and queen meant the same thing,
but to us in our modern terminology it could be said, I
anoint you to become a leader in our Heavenly Father's
kingdom in the government and administration of the degrees of glory after this life is over. So, therefore, we are
testifying of and teaching people the gospel that they may
go into the celestial kingdom.

The Celestial Kingdom of Administration

The celestial kingdom or the kingdom of administration will be the first to be founded and organized, and
those who occupy it are described in the revelations as to
their privilege of early resurrection. "These are they who
are of the Church of the Firstborn." "These are they who
come forth in the morning of the first resurrection," not
the evening. The ones who come in the evening of the first
resurrection will no doubt go into the terrestrial degree.
But those who come in the morning will go into the celestial degree. And then the first resurrection will be over,
and the second resurrection will be for those of the telestial

degree of glory and the sons of perdition, all according to the plan of the gospel of Jesus Christ.[46]

An Analogy

Now let's put it another way. Suppose that we were a group of businessmen who had decided to invest money in a great business involving millions and millions of dollars and the hiring of several hundred thousand workers as we can see in some industries in America. What would we do? Would we leave a meeting like this of the directors and go out and hire all the people before we had even decided what to make? Would we go out and hire people before we had somebody to preside over them? To supervise them? Or would we build an administrative organization first? And set up an administrative office and appoint superintendents and directors and leaders and then go out with them and set up the organization? Well, that is precisely what we would do. That in a sense, but on a more lofty plane, is the way God is preparing the celestial kingdom as a kingdom of administration? Now let me make reference to one or two scriptures to indicate how this had been revealed to us. The first one I have already referred to in Abraham in the Pearl of Great Price,

> Now the Lord had shown unto me, Abraham, the intelligences that were organized before the world was; and among all these there were many of the noble and great ones;
>
> And God saw these souls that they were good, and he stood in the midst of them, and he said: These I will make my rulers; for he stood among those that were spirits, and he saw that they were good; and he said unto me: Abraham, thou art one of them; thou wast chosen before thou wast born.[47]

Everyone of the blood of Israel who has come into the Church is foreordained to that position and calling as a member of the Church—every single one! Every bishop of the Church is foreordained to be a bishop before he

---

[46]See D&C 76:64, 85.
[47]P. of G. P., Abraham 3:22-23.

left the pre-existence. Recently before ordaining several bishops, the writer reminded them that this was the culmination of something that started in the pre-existence when they were chosen of God in the councils of heaven to be bishops in the Church, and that they could take joy in the realization that they had come to that time in their lives when that step was being fulfilled—foreordained to it, and now they were being called to become bishops. In the same sense that we are foreordained to be priests and kings and leaders and administrators, the day will come in the proper time, if we are faithful, that we will be called up to assume these positions of responsibility.

Of the celestial kingdom, we are told,

> They are they who are of the church of the Firstborn.
> They are they into whose hands the Father has given all things—[48]

What do we mean by all things? All knowledge, all power to lead and direct as exists in the presence of God. Not the great power that he has, but the power and influence that emanates from his presence that we may function in it, and as administrators carry on our work. They that are priests and kings who have received of his fulness and of his glory, and he makes them equal in power and in might and in dominion. What do you mean by dominion? Leadership—to govern, control, and direct, and here you have the revelation concerning the terrestrial kingdom which makes this very plain:

> These are they who receive of his glory, but not of his fulness.
> These are they who receive of the presence of the Son, but not of the fulness of the Father.[49]

In other words, Christ will visit and will administer through the priesthood of God in the terrestrial kingdom, but they who are there will not dwell in the fulness of the

---

[46]D&C 76:54-55.
[48]Ibid., 76:76-77.

Father, or have the right of dominion. And of the terrestrial and telestial continuing in the same section:

> These are they who receive not of his fulness in the eternal world, but of the Holy Spirit through the ministration of the terrestrial;
>
> And the terrestrial through the ministration of the celestial.
>
> And also the telestial receive it of the administering of angels who are appointed to minister for them, or who are appointed to be ministering spirits for them; for they shall be heirs of salvation.[50]

John the Revelator was an administering angel. And God shall designate those for the celestial kingdom who shall be called to govern and control and set up the kingdom that will exist in the telestial world in accordance with these revelations. Now further in section 84, verse 33, the great revelation on priesthood, we read:

> For whoso is faithful unto the obtaining these two priesthoods of which I have spoken, and the magnifying their calling, are sanctified by the Spirit unto the renewing of their bodies.
>
> They become the sons of Moses and of Aaron and the seed of Abraham, and the church and kingdom, and the elect of God.
>
> And also all they who receive this priesthood receive me, saith the Lord;
>
> For he that receiveth my servants receiveth me;
>
> And he that receiveth me receiveth my Father;
>
> And he that receiveth my Father receiveth my Father's kingdom; therefore all that my Father hath shall be given unto him.[51]

The Administration of the Glories

Thus we read of the powers of dominion. The telestial receives its administration from the terrestrial where the presence of the Son will govern and under whose direction the priesthood after the order of the Son will

---

[50]*Ibid.*, 86-88.
[51]*Ibid.*, 84:33-38.

administer unto this kingdom, as well as also the administering angels from the celestial kingdom. (See D&C 7.) John the Apostle is an administering apostle unto the heirs of salvation. These of the celestial kingdom as referred to, no doubt, directed by the Christ will administer and govern the lesser glories. In all of this we see a purpose. Everyone of us dwelt in the pre-existence with God and was given a challenge of leadership, and privileged to come to earth at this particular time to fulfil that challenge and prove worthy of further leadership appointment in the continuing plan of the gospel.

A Question of Birth

Have you ever wondered why you were born today instead of 2000 years ago? Did this just happen or was there something organized about it? Why weren't you born in the days of Moses instead of today? What were the processes in the pre-existence that permitted you as an individual spirit to come into the world in this day? In the light of our understanding the answers to these important questions are clear. It is simply that this is the day of birth that you merited. Thus your entrance into mortality at this latter day was purposeful and foreordained. As missionaries go throughout the world as part of that withholding until the last dispensation, sent to proclaim the gospel of Jesus Christ unto the gentiles and as many of the house of Israel as shall be called. To prepare them for entrance into the kingdom of our Heavenly Father: First, here upon earth, and secondly, through proven worthiness that they may become priests, kings, and rulers to assist our Heavenly Father in preparing the kingdom of administration that will govern and control the other kingdoms which will be eternally above those in the terrestrial and telestial kingdoms.

A Person of Nobility

All of this is according to the great plan of salvation that makes of each of us a very, very important person.

The power of individuality is not to be spoken of in a sense of egotism, not in a sense of lifting ourselves up in pride, but actually as members of his Church and kingdom here upon earth as we contemplate our pre-existent position of having been withheld in mortal birth to come forth in this great period of time to proclaim the gospel, to give over and over again our witness of the truth and to otherwise assist our Heavenly Father in the work. This makes of us a person of nobility, and if this were not so we would not be as we are today, members of the Church and the servants of God.

Now, if we by some miracle had the power to see each other in our true spiritual form, some of our spirits would be a little bigger than our bodies. I have often thought as I have looked at some of our short missionaries, and we observe the example sometimes of a tall missionary and a short one. But it just might be the opposite in the next world. Because we don't know the dimensional sizes of our spirits. It is felt, however, that not all of our spirits are of the same size. I presume that a spirit is full-grown when it enters the body of a child. In some way, not understood, this tiny body is superimposed with the spirit, and as the body grows in its image, unless it is curtailed by physical weakness, disease or accident, it will undoubtedly grow to the form of the spirit. But oftentimes disease creeps in; children at birth have accidents, causing a physical injury to some part of the body which affects proper growth. A brother called to an important Church position recently was observed to have a back deformity, his legs were abnormally longer than the trunk of his body. But in that man is a glorified spirit. It has no deformity, but his spirit must go along with that body until the body dies, for the spirit cannot leave the body until the body dies. The spirit cannot remain with a mortal body that has ceased to function and when this occurs, the spirit departs and thus at once exists in the spirit world which without doubt is a part of this life.

The day of this life is from the day you were born until the end of the period of the spirit world. It is not at the end of this mortal life. This is why we preach the gospel in the spirit world so that the work can be done for people vicariously here upon the earth, within the recognized day of this life.

In the day of resurrection, when the elements of the physical or mortal body are to again become an eternal part of the complete image, it will then grow to the full stature of the spirit, this in accordance with the principles of the resurrection. There will be no deformities. The arms and the body will be perfect with its characteristics of personality.

We look at people and see many of them with one arm or one leg, and if we want to look closer still we will see them with two to four layers of leather on their shoes to compensate for the fact that one leg is shorter than the other. And there are many other observable deformities. Sometimes we hear of a person referred to as ugly caused by the contour of the face, which, while perserving parental characteristics, takes on the appearance of ugliness because of the tricks of nature, wherein a cheekbone is caused to protrude from the face, or the chin bones to recede and thus the face grows lopsided. One eye may be lower than another, or in numerous other ways the growth of physical parts of the body may be abnormal; then we say that person is ugly. But the time will come in the resurrection when that face or body will have its proper form and proportions and there will be no ugliness. There is no ugliness now if we will look at the real person, at his spirit and not at his physical appearances.

Unto those who are born into a lesser kingdom in this life there can come an improvement to their place; for example, the day will come when the Negro will receive the gospel and will have the opportunity to receive the priesthood also. The time will come when the Jews will be redeemed and be relieved of that curse which is upon them for the crucifixion of the Christ. The time will come when the Lamanites will be made a white and delightsome people, and their backwardness and their lack of memory and all of the traits of character which are now placed upon them will vanish. Many of the American Indians are evidencing these signs of returning to their status before the curse was placed upon them. But in South and Central America we see the lower castes of the descendants of the Nephites and Lamanites. The day, however, will come when they also will rise from that, which was placed upon them. In time they will be relieved from the curse which came upon them because of their rejection of the prophets and their proclaiming of the gospel of Jesus Christ unto them. These three divisions of cursed people that have had a judgment placed upon them, some of whom were of chosen lineages, indicate that in the plan of agency, man must constantly be in the light.

Now back to the people in the second division that I spoke of—the gentile. This is their day. They are having the opportunities to improve their place from one position to another. But at the end of this life, at the end of the spirit world, then there can be no change. And they must do their changing here in this probation. The Prophet Alma explains this, as found in the 34th chapter of Alma in the Book of Mormon, beginning with the 31st verse.

> Yea, I would that ye would come forth and harden not your hearts any longer; for behold, now is the time and the day of your salvation; and therefore, if ye will repent and harden not your hearts, immediately shall the great plan of redemption be brought about unto you.[52]

Our great responsibility as missionaries is to lead people to repentance, for when a person repents, yielding to the influence of a servant of God who testifies to them, then the whole plan of salvation opens unto him and he understands it. Somewhere in the secret caverns of himself he understands the gospel message too. Men were

---

[52]Alma 34:31.

taught it in the pre-existence. They may even have a greater knowledge of it than we do. Alma tells us that if they will only repent under the direction of the servants of God, that immediately the great plan of redemption will be brought back to their understanding.

With this knowledge at hand, our obligation as members of the kingdom of our Heavenly Father is diligently to proclaim these truths unto other people. Continuing the writings of Alma,

> For behold, this life is the time for men to prepare to meet God; yea, behold the day of this life is the day for men to perform their labors.[53]

And now this is the particular scripture that I want to call attention to:

> And now, as I said unto you before, as ye have had so many witnesses, therefore, I beseech of you that ye do not procrastinate the day of your repentance until the end; for after this day of life, (which is from birth until the end of the spirit world) which is given us to prepare for eternity, behold, if we do not improve our time (if we do not improve our place) while in this life, then cometh the night of darkness wherein there can be no labor performed.[54]

And so the Lord in his love, in his kindness, thought to make of this probation another opportunity for his spirit children to come to know the gospel. All of the preaching and all of the influences and powers of persuasion that could have been used were used upon us in the pre-existence, and all who were noble and valiant have there been chosen, and those of the medium division were chosen and those in the lesser division were appointed. But now here in this life, which is a probation, men have the opportunity to move from the lower division to a higher division. That is why a Negro born in this life, imposed with a judgment in the pre-existence to a lower division,

---

[53]*Ibid.*, 34:32.
[54]*Ibid.*, 34:33.

may, by receiving the gospel, be elevated to the higher division. And the same with others who are born in the second division: they too may advance.

But in all probations, there is also a danger of a down grade and those who come into this life to a noble position may lose their place and end up in the terrestrial kingdom or in the telestial, or even become a son of perdition. This is the very point of the plan of free agency that Lucifer no doubt grasped and tried to get sufficient support to destroy the plan. He wanted to save everyone under the principle of force, to be accomplished as he proposed by eliminating agency that all who would go into this world would come back into the spirit world in their same station. There would be no change. This had a great influence upon many, for a third of the hosts of heaven believed him and followed his erroneous and destructive way. Actually Satan's plan was deception and could not happen as he must have claimed it would.

This same principle of the plan is conveyed in Christ's parable of the talents. With the one who did not want to take a chance on losing his place, and he who was given one talent buried it. Do you get the true meaning of the parable of the talents? The consequence of this is that all of life is depicted in this very parable which the Christ speaks of in the assigning of the five talents, representing the children of the noble lineage, the assigning of the two, of the adopted lineage, and the assigning of the one, of the lower lineage. This is all a part of the organized plan of the gospel of Jesus Christ. There was a chosen people in the pre-existence. Literally there was an Israel in heaven and in the procreation of man. Those same spirits were born through such channels as to be given the opportunity, now, again to prove themselves, while those of lesser kingdoms were to have the opportunity to elevate themselves from one kingdom to another. But as Alma has stated, after the day of this life then there can be no work done for them.

Now, in conclusion, here is a summarization. That all men are created equal, may be true in a political sense, for such laws as men may provide for the protection of the individual rights on the basis of equality and opportunity; of course, we recognize no discriminating influence. But if applied as meaning that all men are born with equal capacity or even with inherent abilities, in like measure for each, such becomes absurd and manifestly false. Every spirit born in the flesh is an individual character and brings to the body prepared for its tenancy, a nature all of its own, fashioned and made ready by its degree of advancement in the pre-existent state referred to by the Lord as the *first estate*. The principle of agency provides that tendencies, likes, and dislikes, in fact, the entire make-up of the spirit may be intensified or changed by the course of mortal life, and thus the spirit may advance or retrogress while allied with its mortal tabernacle.

Man shall, therefore, conclude his mortal probation or *second estate* to that degree of achievement made possible by the *combination of his pre-existent level visited upon him in mortal birth and with that which he is able to do with himself here in this life.* Therefore, the sum and substance of his place in that stage of life to follow this one, referred to as the stage of glory, will be the combination of both the first estate and the second.

Here are the states of existence; there are four conditions and stages in the advancement of the individual soul as made known to us by divine revelation. They are:

1. *The Unembodied* or the spirit world.
2. *The Embodied,* when men take upon themselves a body in this life.
3. *The Disembodied,* when there is a brief separation of the spirit and the mortal body awaiting the resurrection.
4. *The Resurrected.*

In other words, (A) every one of us lived in a premortal existence as an individual spirit. (B) We are now advanced to the stage of mortal existence, in which we have taken a mortal body. (C) We shall live in a disembodied state after death, which is but a separation of the body and the spirit. (D) And in due time each one of us, whether righteous or sinful, shall be resurrected from the dead with spirit and body being reunited, never again to be separated.

In the plan of salvation, which has been made known to us in this dispensation, through the revelations given to the Prophet Joseph Smith, we are privileged to perceive and understand the principle of foreordination. In a footnote from the *Articles of Faith* (Lecture 10, Article 5) by Dr. James E. Talmage, we are enlightened by the following article from the book entitled *A Compendium of the Doctrines of the Gospel* written by Franklin D. Richards and James A. Little, under the heading of Foreordination:

> The writings of the book of Genesis in the Bible, and from Moses and Abraham in the Pearl of Great Price make it plain that man existed in a spiritual condition prior to coming here, and also quite as evident that in that pre-existence be exercised his free agency. God may have called and chosen man in their first estate, or spiritual existence, but whether they will accept that call and fill it, by repentance and good works in this life, is a matter in which it is their privilege to exercise their free agency. Men exercised their free agency in the first or spiritual estate, as well as in this. *That the character of their works in that estate shaped their destiny in this is evident.*[55]

And in conclusion, let me say this, as expressed by a non-Mormon.

> Mormonism as a theory offers the most comprehensive and consistent explanation of the great mystery of life.

Then in the book, "The Outlines of Mormon Philosophy" we read this,

> What thoughtful man must long for is some firm center about which he can organize his knowledge of

---

[55]*Compendium of the Doctrines of the Gospel,* see Foreordination.

the world, his experiences of life, a point of view from which he can gather all into an intelligible unity, and with which he can press forward with a deep assurance of divine guidance and adequate outcome.

May the Lord bless us all and help us to appreciate the fact that servants of God divinely committed to go forth with the assistance of our Heavenly Father in bringing about his purposes, are preparing men and women to be leaders in his kingdoms, at the same time working out their own salvation seeking to fulfil their destinies as priests and kings and as queens and priestesses in the eternal realms of our Heavenly Father.

INDEX